Behind Grey Curtains
MICAL Confidential

By
P. Carl Gibson

For information, email to: betcgreen@gmail.com

For information about special discounts for bulk purchases please contact email address aforementioned.

For more information or to book an event contact the above email and there information could be had about the same.

Dedication

To Aunty Rosez & Dada.
Whose critical insights and thoughts
Into the possibilities will always be remembered.

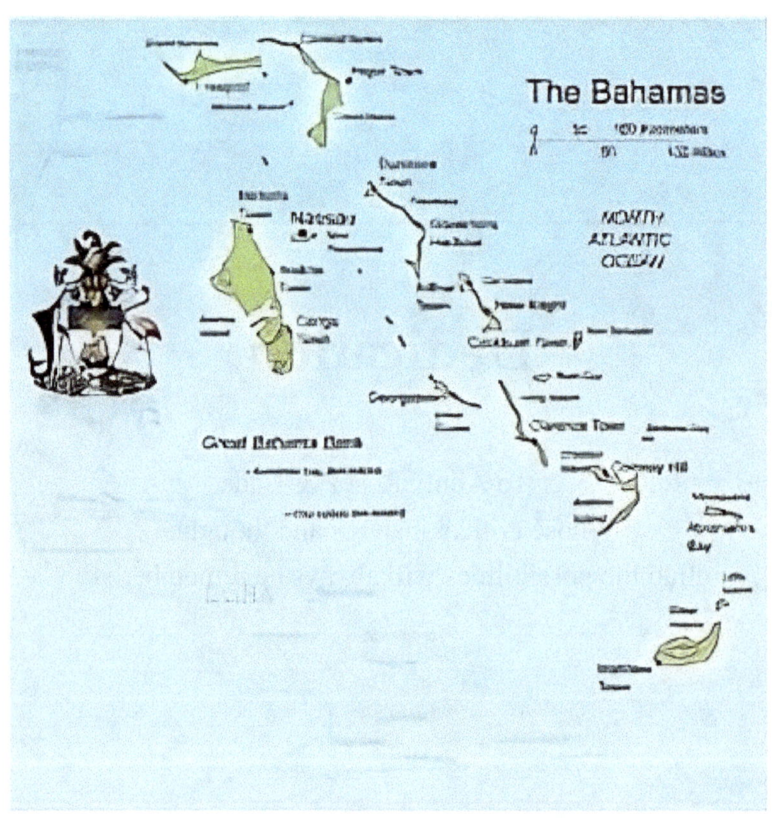

The islands of the Bahamas.

Acknowledgement

There has never been another historical crisis of the magnitude in the Bahamas from 1956 -2004 in which so many people were keenly interested.

Capt. Daniel Gibson 2008

I live everyday perpetually conscious of all the people who made life a reality for me.

As the Lord lives, I am grateful for each person who encouraged and supported my hopes and dreams that really gave these thoughts shape.

I am forever indebted to my mother and father for their steel like integrity and diligence to duty and love for country as they encouraged me to ask questions and to dig deep into my soul and question why we were called "Children behind Gods' back," and the belief that someday a great light would shine on all the children of the southern chain of islands in the Bahamas and time slipped into the future.

Esther Wilkerson who always suggested that I pick up a book and read.

Mildred Williamson who taught all the children under her care, to never take 'no' as an answer when one had to climb up a hill to finish any task.

Julia Jones who helped raised many of the little boys children in Pirates Well and toiled daily with a bucket on her head as she sung "God will take care of you. All of you." Every day as she walked jovially past the native folks who always call out to her as "Granny."

Uncle Leonard Murphy who taught me to fish and how to pull in the fishing line with the first barracuda I caught in his small dingy on his way to "Bubby cay off the coast of the island of Mayaguana, Bahamas.

Rodney Collie who told me and many other youth men to always question authority particularly when it involved the history of the nation; but then Rodney Collie ascended to never be seen again.

That was long ago and one of the foremost of days I can recall in my life. But they said that God is God and God is just. I never understood.

Sister Roselene, aunty Laura, aunty Effie and uncle Leonards' wife who almost singlehandedly told every young person they came in contact with to always be "respectful and to honor always "old people."

Pastor Alexander Brown would remind me whenever he picked me up in his pickup truck to do errands with him around the church that it was better to stay simple and honest with everything we do.

Constable Louie Williamson who was an iron clad man of lawfulness who did not take anyone for granted but executed the law fairly and respectfully.

Also Silas Savage who made it his business to take me to hear Adam Clayton Powell (U.S.A) 1972 speeches; on Seventh Avenue in New York City and then registered me to work as a canvasser in the election of Jimmy Carter in 1975 – 1976.

Silas Savage showed me why civic involvement by citizens was mandatory for democratic successes to take root and grow.

I am never going to forget to talk about these people who gave me a voice and an identity with strength to speak up when in doubt and the others I would not have enough ink to write their names.

To Russell Saunders of Kansas City Missouri, who was always so authentic, kind and stood as a confidant as I sought the truth and justice to define oneself.

Russell Saunders always say out loud and firmly; "Donot let any one influene you...Ok?

I never forgot that when I started to visit the Garage and Studio 54 and other large party venues.

To Ucal McPhee with whom I shared jokes and chatted about what could become vibrant and economically strong southeastern islands of Mayaguana and Inagua Bahamas.

In recognition of what lies ahead in the midst of all the despair, one must be true to oneself no matter what it curved into.

Content

Let It Be

With a large bowl of conch salad, a cooler of ice and two shopping bags loaded with soft island beverages. I looked out from the second floor balcony of a beachfront hotel on New Providence island, Bahamas and heard clearly the noise in the marketplace from political voices belching phrases like, "Things have never been better; " and "Everyone is doing fine just fine… you know?"

You still hear some say; "Look even America have the same problems too ... even worst!"

While clear out of nowhere, someone hollered; "We funded temporary benefits for the unemployed."

Then someone coughed out; "Give us another chance."

True story as their motive seems clearly slanted and varied.

I wondered whether these comments were made as an attempt to dim any pressing need to answer direct questioning of party dogmas or key policy designs on national issues relevant to the new and evolving Bahamas narrative on economic, cultural, national security, physical disability and elder care along with public transportation, agriculture and infrastructure development throughout the islands from being aired and drafted.

Frankly the myth of "Keeping the islands like it always been," has been a verbal assault on island-wide consistent progressive growth.

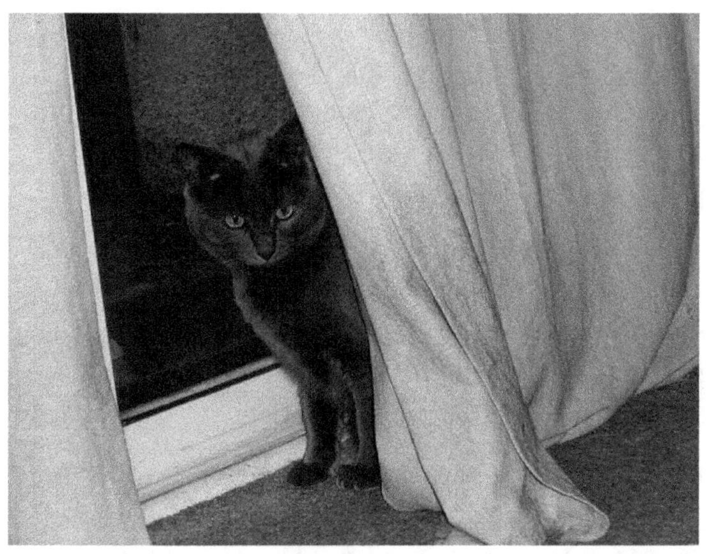

Dada scanning the view

Examples are numerous:

Public transportation spending could open steady growth as a "fixed asset" in a balance sheet" moving forward.

"Fixed Assets" turnover, infra-structure and prosperity may echo fabulous growth for the country well into the century.

Thereby through defined economic expansion throughout the islands likely, these and any targeted investments could cushion the economy from downward recessionary trends looming and the tourism dependence path.

While being mindful this may also help set in place long term growth and also provides a revenue stream that could generate funds for needed social services continuum.

What images do transportation in New Providence Bahamas conjures in the mind of an average traveler?

Probably drivers on the left side of the street and highway hastily moving sometimes to nowhere or just standing still on

Blue hill road, Market street or Soldier road to East street and then I remembered some people were saying "It's better in the Bahamas," with years of television commercials some showing beautiful beaches with mostly tourists swimming with dolphins, sharks and stingrays, enjoying Gods' creation far away from their home without any care or worry......and we sung "This land is my land, from Great Inagua to Grand Bahama! " but then I remained stuck in traffic on the east west highway and sing and sing and sung hoping soon public transportation will be introduced as a remedy for the congested crowded streets.

Take a look at the privately owned "public used" buses or jitney transportation flowchart that is allowed to foment on the island of New Providence, which do move residents throughout the island and put a limited number of the bus owners and companies in a revenue stream.

Note well, "Benefits limited number of bus owners" – while hardly contributing to social services or the human resources of the islands' people, neither does it generates revenue for any of the local government initiatives.

Such is the case and may be worthwhile for what it does.

There is no questioning of that fact.

The movement of people in and around the islands is pivotal and vital for smooth and orderly national security to embrace an "If you see something, say something," open campaign that encourages safety amongst the people and the country every day.

Another may query; should the bus routes be open to competitive bidding?

Emphatically it does look like the country should own and benefit from all land usages or revenue that is generated or accrued from mass transit usages. As workers would in turn contributes in the supply and demand markets in communities and districts on the islands and beyond.

Summarily with some $20.5 to $37.1 million derived from the public using the "jitney" services annually, according to some sources on the island of New Providence suggests 'resident benefits' are none nor does it provide services to the community at large in many ways?

Examples are numerous like, senior citizens' prescription drugs costs, school lunches, after school training, national services, educational and mentoring and other pivotally observed needed services from fees for road usages assigned for infrastructure development.

So is the country benefitting in any way as we know it from the "publicly, used" privately owned bus system that roam the streets and highways of the island regulated or not regulated?

The answer is unequivocal.

Little revenue is now derived from the growth or the fomenting of this system as we presently see, observed and should it be changed and nationalized and owned by the people for the people?

Then should the system be expanded into a new vibrant national "comprehensive transit system" (CTS), with so called, "Bah cards" used on all public transit systems for daily, weekly, monthly and other specialty travel?

Yes, it should be clearly established for a continued betterment while enhancing the national integrity of the public transportation system as used by the public.

Safety and national security are compromised when public transportation is questionable.

Bah. card:

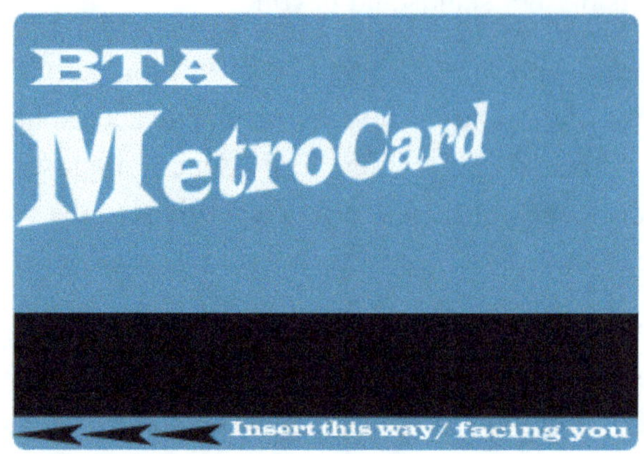

Bahcard 2026 (Front view)

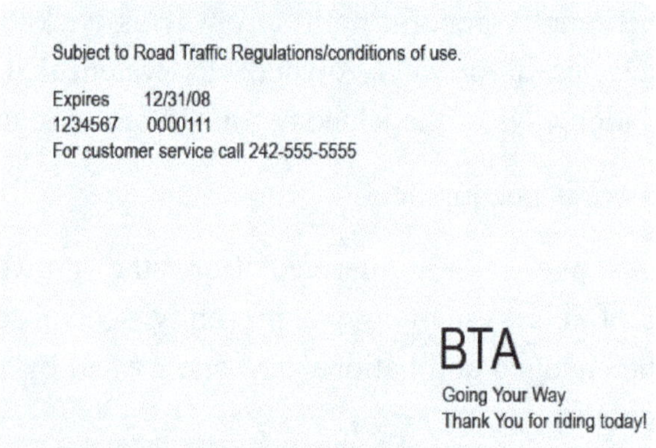

Bah card 2026 (Back view)

These are questions needed to be answered as imminent concerns for an orderly, perpetual and synchronized public transportation system to emerged and be nationalized.

This may spell an ideal quality of life change for all once nationalization is realized.

Note there are multiple options associated with various routes that may be leased and or open to market manipulations.

Another pivotal issue is investors may be courted and scouted in earnest for infrastructure development, which they will no doubt miss a giant opportunity if they avoid the looming potential in the islands of the Bahamas for massive growth with an upsurge in world economic outlook.

There are other compelling and endless trends in the Bahamas for the economy to grow and expand at a tiger like rate of 2.5 percent to 5.0 percent pace.

Bahamas' highways, roads and privately owned "public transportation system" contribute to virtually everything of value in the economy and the day to day functionality of all the people's lives – from linking business to their suppliers and customers, to bringing jobs, education, health care, recreation , or just taking a ride to town and government services being within every nationals' reach .

A country, town or city is only as good as it transit system. That's really why continued vital investments in new technology, equipments and infrastructure are encouraged for the future to be bright and profoundly cheerful.

Economists have explored the economic impact of public investment for decades and have consistently found that surface transportation systems increase economic output, reduce prices and raise incomes and profits.

Investing in this extensive network has produced enormous economic returns for virtually every person and businesses in the country.

Again with mass usage of this system which has to be designed to fit and comply and conform with perceived national security concerns and seamlessly integrating into an organized and well functioning part of a carefully structured Bahamian system.

If you see something say something is a vital tool for safety and public awareness maintenance at all times.

With visionary development and economic expansion, the next twenty years could lift the nation and the children for generations to come.

Again even with economic growth even at a rate of 1.5 percent to 3.5 percent annually, investors may find banks, supermarket outfits, new mobile phone and media companies with excellent prospects.

A country, town, or city is only as good as it transit system. That's really why continued vital investments in new technology, equipment and infrastructure are encouraged for the future to be bright and profoundly gainful.

Also the building of seaports, power plants, sewer plants, highways, roads, tunnel construction and other capital infrastructure projects are most favorable to sustain valiant gross domestic product (gdp) growth throughout the island nation chain with impressive national potential.

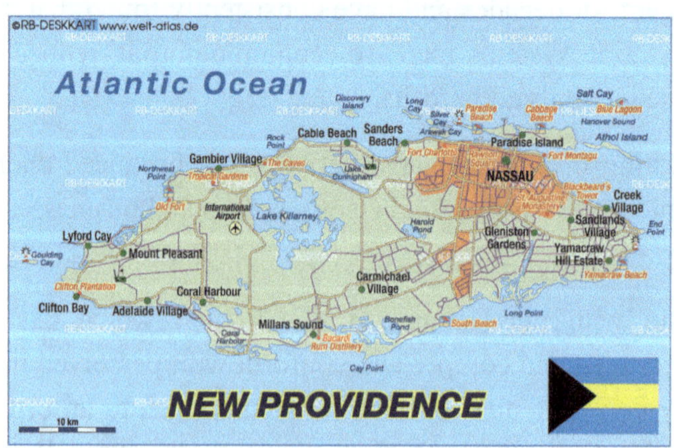

New Providence Bahamas island.

Papa's Story

Look inside the country

Look all around the islands

The islands are changing fast

But is it moving in the

Right direction?

.........Bulla Danny - 1979

The Commonwealth of the Bahamas (known as the Bahamas); since the birth of independence July 10 1973, has yet to organize a "Comprehensive Public Transportation" system (CPT) to benefit and safeguard the integrity of mass transportation for the people Nassau Bahamas 2016 and beyond with a complete setup of a comprehensive system of transportation and other likely organized Shock & Awe Economic and National Development (S&AED) proposals.

Today the public system is owned and operated by a number of families who has performed a great service for the riding public.

However, the "Authorities", have to seriously consider the needs of the people as a whole and advance a "Comprehensive mass transit" system which will benefit all the people of the country with the introduction of the Bahamas Transit Authority (BTA):

This system will be able to pay for itself in a matter of three to seven years and could render the family or privately owned bus enterprises obsolete and services deemed vital to the needs of the people may prosper and grow: e.g. : a. Public education (b) People with disability and Senior citizen meals on wheels.

Here is an example of how this system should work and could be upgraded to facilitate the growing numbers of potential riders.

Route 1 - Bay Street - from the Straw market as we know it should see improvement(s) to accommodate the growing number of riders throughout the island of New Providence.

A new and up-to-date bus terminal where it all began and or end.

Route 2 - East street going south - from Windsor park bus (es) going in both directions.

Route 3 - East street from Windsor park going to Shirley street - ONE WAY street immediately.

Route 4 - Wulff both directions bus(es) to accommodate riders of ALL bus(es) with an option to give free Transfers to be used on bus(es) on Route 1, 2, 3, and 4.

Route 5 - Wulff road / beginning at Collins avenue to Shirley street bus(es) in both directions to accommodate riders with bus transfers to be used on Route 1, 2, 3, & 4.

Route 6 - Mackey street / beginning at Porter cay/ East Bay street bus(es) in both directions.

Route 7 - Robinson road in both directions / beginning @ Blue hill/Yellow Elder park area going to a specified region up to Fox Hill with transfers for bus(es) going to Route H which will cover Soldier road in both directions crossing East street with transfers for bus(es) going to Route1 (note well) East street in both directions.

Now Kennedy subdivision may have shuttle bus(es) to Soldier road both directions with transfers applicable.

Malcombe road east and west with shuttle bus (es) to connect with above mentioned route(s).

Carmichael road from Blue Hill road both directions called Route P with connection to other sub-divisions in the region.

Frequently Asked Questions: (FAQ)

1. How would BTA be comprised?

The BTA would have the responsibility for developing and implementing a unified mass movement of people in the islands of the Bahamas.

2. How much would be the bus ride cost?

Somewhere like $1.50 - $2.00

3. Would the drivers be allowed to play music on the buses?

No.

4. Would the government buy out the presently private bus owners?

That could be under the wide range of discussion

5. Are the bus drivers paid by the treasury or what?

The drivers will be paid by BTA. Bahamas Transit Authority.

6   Would there be a BTA bus card?

YES

7. Where would cards be purchased?

At assigned outlets and at bus depots.

8. What would happen to all the buses now on the road?

They would be retired and taken off the road.

9. Would BTA be a quasi-government owned corporation?

Yes that could be one of the designed options.

10. How would people with disability be accommodated?

Buses will be fitted with lifting or kneeing apparatus.

11. What would it cost people with disability?

Somewhere around half the price as determined.

12. What time would the buses start and end?

From 4.00 a.m. to 1.00 a.m. daily until further notice.

13 How much would be half fare for people with disability?

Half the price of regular bus users.

14. Would drivers be able to join unions?

Yes or an option to be explored.

15. Would the public support BTA?

YES! The general public would be supportive once advertised adequately and riders would speak of the improvements and gains appropriately .

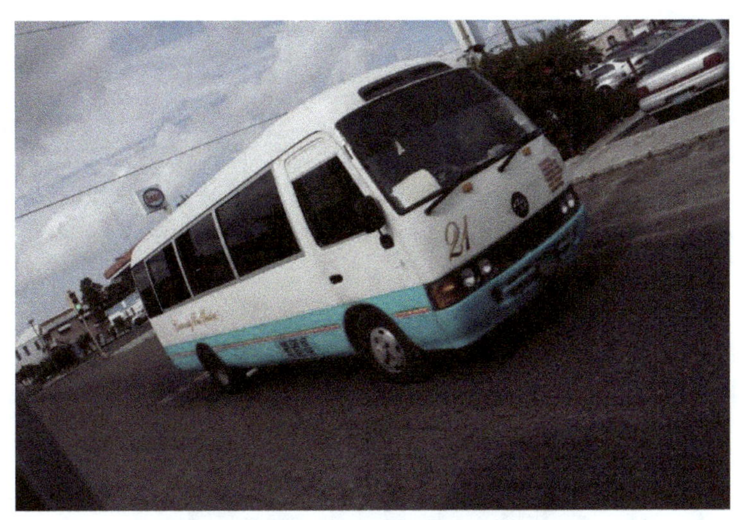

Local Bus no: 21 that ply the island of
New Providence Bahamas.

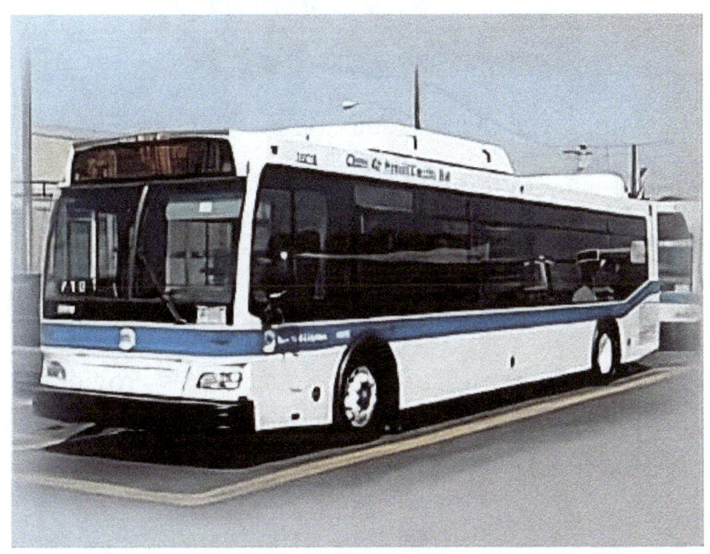

(Electric powered buses to carry more than 50 -100 persons
at a time).

Sir Roland Symonette

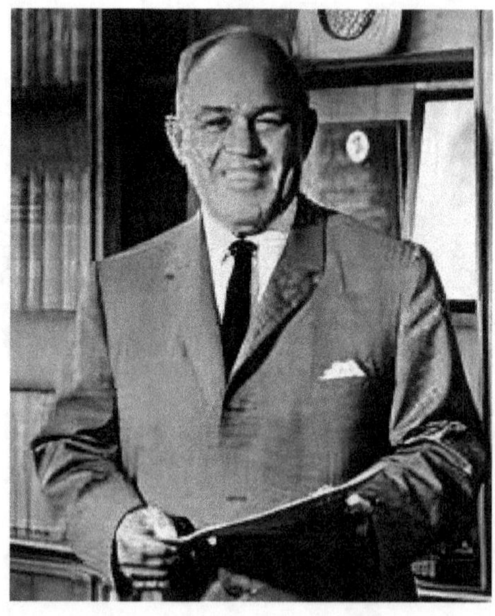

Chief Minister of the Bahamas 1955 – 1959

Also Known As: "Pop Symonette"

Birthdate: December 16, 1898

Birthplace: The Current, North Eleuthera, the Bahamas

Death: Died March 13, 1980 in Nassau, New Providence, the Bahamas Cause of death: Complications of pancreatic cancer Place of Burial: Nassau, New Providence, The Bahamas

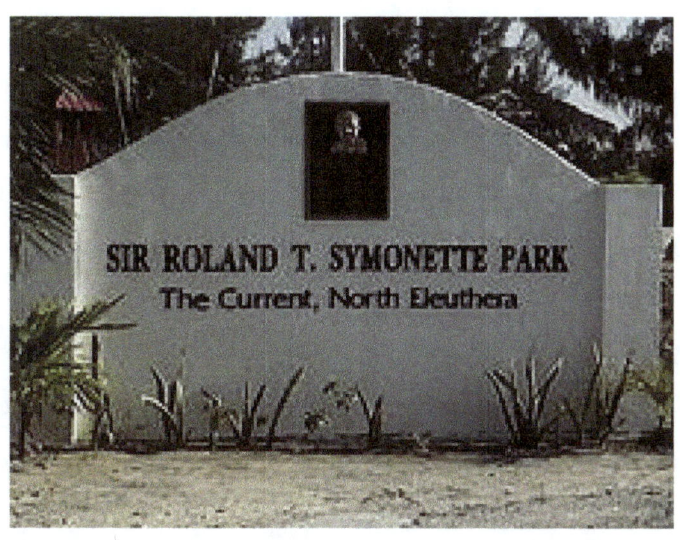

1st Premier of the Bahamas

In office January 1964 - January 1967

Born   16 December 1898
            Current, Eleuthera

Died   13 March 1980 (age 81)

Sir Roland Theodore Symonette (16 December 1898–13 March 1980) achieved high office as a Bahamian political figure.

Roland "Pop" Symonette was born on the small island settlement of Current, Eleuthera. Symonette was one of many children of Methodist Minister Edwin Symonette and his wife Lavania (née Weech).

Although he had no known formal education, Sir Roland Symonette became one of the wealthiest men of his generation. A self taught and life-long advocate of education, Sir Roland Symonette was a school teacher early in his career, but, during Prohibition, Sir Roland Symonette 'ran' rum to the United States. With the profits from rum-running, Sir Roland Symonette invested in real estate, liquor stores and, eventually, a shipyard. The Symonette family's holdings have never been publicly confirmed, but public speculation has placed it between $700 million and $2.5 billion (US).

In 1925, Sir Roland Symonette campaigned successfully for a seat in the Bahamas' House of Assembly. Symonette served in the House, representing the Shirlea district, without interruption until his retirement in 1977. Symonette's fifty two years as a member of Parliament is the longest record of service in the House of Assembly.

Sir Roland Symonette served as the head of government of the Bahama islands from 1955 to 1964 and in 1964, when the country achieved internal self-government; Sir Roland Symonette became the first Premier of the Bahama Islands. In 1959, Symonette was knighted by Queen Elizabeth II.

Sir Roland Symonette was married three times. By his first wife Nellie, he had one son, Basil Harcourt. By his second wife, the former Thelma Bell Clepper of Andalusia, Alabama, he had a one son, Robert "Bobby" and one daughter, Zelda. In the late 1940s, he married Canadian Margaret Frances. This third marriage produced one daughter, Margaret, who died in infancy, and two sons, Roland Craig and Brent. Sir Roland

Symonette's son Bobby served formerly as Speaker of the House of Assembly. His youngest son Brent Symonette is the current Deputy Prime Minister of The Bahamas, Free National Movement and Minister of Foreign Affairs in the Ingraham led government.

Sir Roland Symonette died on 13 March 1980 at his home in Nassau; his widow, Lady Margaret Symonette died twenty-four years later in 2004.

Sir Roland Symonette's portrait appears on the Bahamian fifty dollar note.

The community park in the settlement of Current, Eleuthera, Bahamas just feet away from where Sir. Roland was born was named and commemorated in his Honor on what would have been his 111 birthday on December 16, 2009. On hand for the dedication ceremony were Sir Roland's two sons, the Hon. Brent Symonette, Deputy Prime Minister of the Bahamas, and his brother Mr. Craig Symonette, a well accomplished businessman, along with their families.

In Memory of Things Past:

From the days of 'Noah' native Bahamians knew of Sir Randol Fawkes who made it his duty to challenge the dominant authorities of his time while laboring faithfully for better employment and working conditions for all inhabitants of the country.

Meanwhile the day seem long as the sun shined brightly at noontime, a handful of cousins sat under a coconut tree and balked about the Rev. Martin Luther King Jr., "I have a dream" speech on Wednesday August 28, 1963.

It was February 1964 a leap year, many islanders thought "someday" Mayaguana and Inagua would be vital to the chain of islands and maybe will no longer 'be behind God's back', as many people surmised.

That breezy Sunday morning, most residents had heard and supported the Gandhi-like, non-violent resistant tactics, as was proclaimed by the reverent gentleman throughout North America.

Some people had already begun to filter into New Providence island to join the voices led by Sir Randol Fawkes for labor rights and fair pay; with Sir Lynden O. Pindling and others focusing on the forces dressed as a United Bahamian Party (U.B.P) government headed by Sir Roland Symonette the former Chief Minister of the Bahamas and his maximum Minister Sir Stafford Sands.

Even though the U.B.P with Sir Roland Sermonette as the Leader stood not only as a government, but a force with many transplanted deep pocket financial explorers and bigots seeking to perpetuate a concept with heavy racial overtones that separated native people by skin color, it did not work very well in the Bahamas experiment.

By now the native Bahamians were hearing much about a non-violent resistance, equal rights and justice, a native preacher named pastor Alexander Brown, kept reminding the congregation that the time had come for Mayaguanian/Inaguian islanders to be "resolute and face the task ahead."

True what the preacher wanted too was running water, paved roads, electricity, public libraries, health clinics, telephone services and regular low cost air and sea travel to New Providence and elsewhere for all citizens of the islands.

Sitting behind gray curtains Mayaguanian/Inaguian islanders knew New Providence residents basked in the glow of flushing bathrooms everywhere so the twin islands sought the same, even as the "outhouse"; sometimes-called latrine was a well-known local fixture was vanishing fast.

The preacher suggested one sunny Sunday morning that a "son of the soil" in Parliament would be helpful to achieve social justice, island wide growth throughout the southeastern corner of the country.

The preacher continued that a voice to advocate in parliament would spearhead efforts to bring employment opportunities and light industries to the southern corner of the Bahamas, near the Turks and Caicos islands where many residents had roots and family history for centuries, long before Blackbeard water hole was dug in Pirates Well, Mayaguana.

Then like now, Mayaguanians/Inaguians knew was, what they still know today as Morton Salt, a lone American based employer which generated multiple paychecks for migrating workers from neighboring islands, helping families to eat food, buy clothes for school children, church services and many practical necessities.

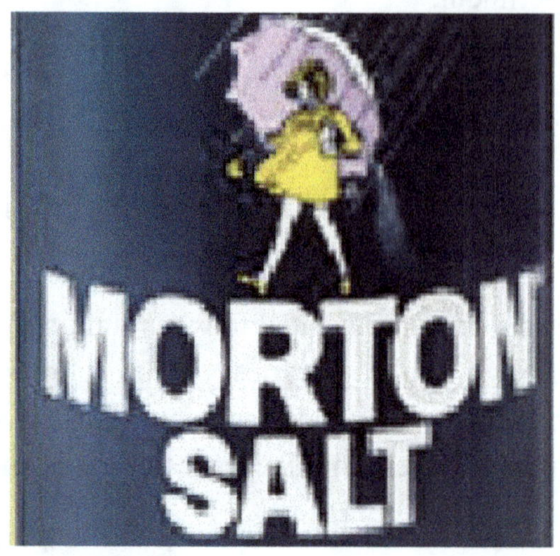

Morton Salt box

We give thanks for Morton salt - Matthew Town Inagua Bahamas.

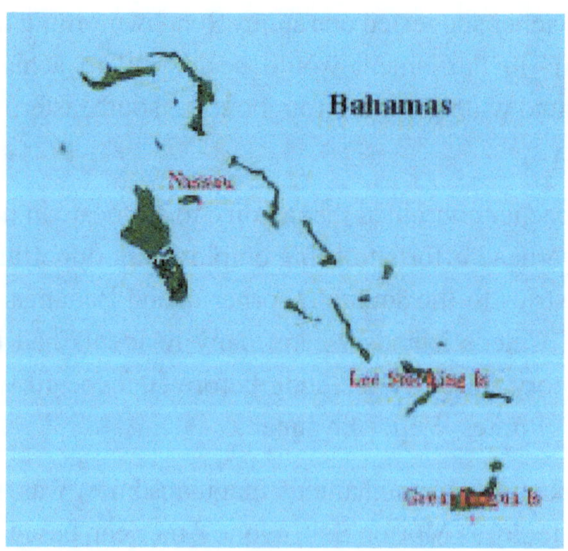

islands of Bahamas

Anyhow, in Pirates Well, Mayaguana, the lone constable drove down the narrow quarry road heading to Betsy bay, greeting everyone by their name.

Many residents loved and knew the constable was doing an excellent job, but was he the "son of the soil" the preacher alluded to, since after all he'd given a big mail boat to ply back and forth to Mayaguana and beyond bringing building materials, heavy equipments and food supplies regularly from Nassau.

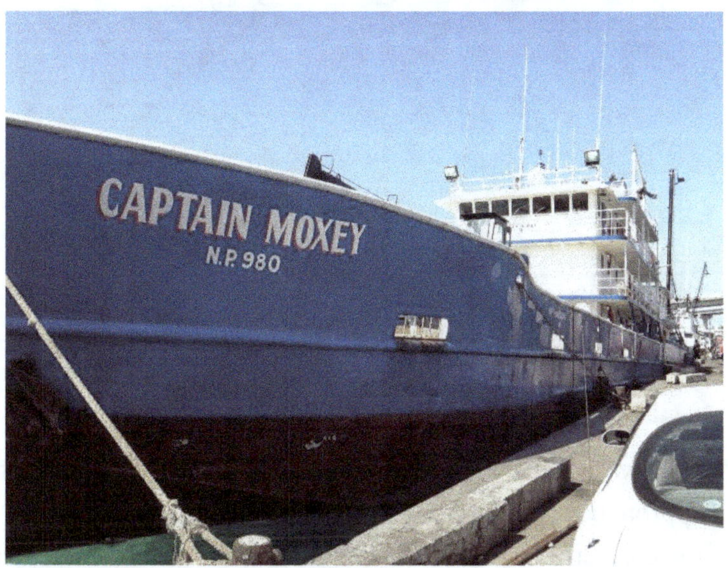

M/V "Captain Moxey" of the South Andros runs leaves New Providence Mondays at 11 p.m. Moxey Shipping with Captain Kevin Moxey. Another skipper is Captain Boycel Moxey Jr., described as a Principal of the company.

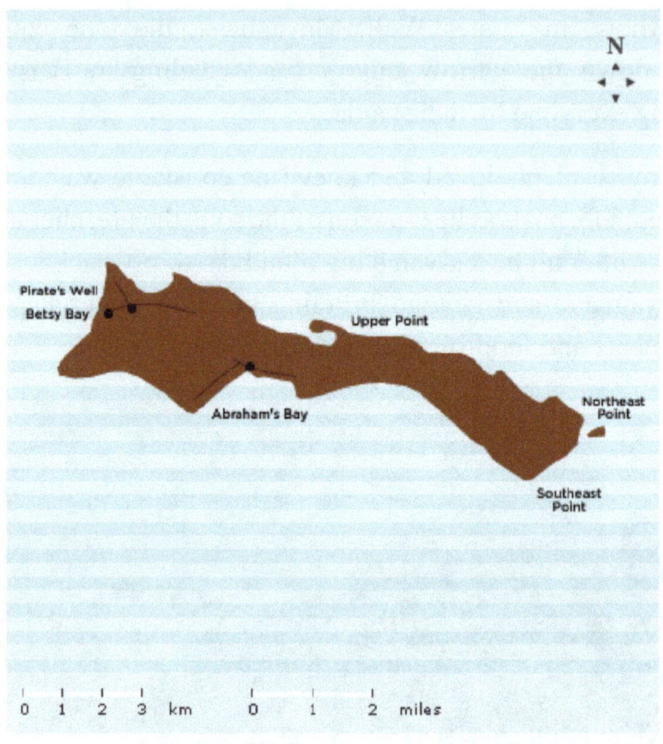

Mayaguana island Bahamas

"Time would tell," the elder man would always say, as lunch time approached; British overseas airline (BOAC) was seen over the horizon on the way to the large airbase not far from Abraham's bay, the capital town of the island.

As in Pirates Well and neighboring upper bay area many residents had been preparing to go to the evangelical church this time for a prayer meeting, as news flashed on ZNS radio Bahamas community announcements, requesting a group of long time anchored inhabitants of Mayaguana who lived on New Providence island to report to Yellow Elder primary school.

This was for an organized meeting called for notables like Mr. Freeman McPhee, Miss Linda Collie, Miss Roselene Gibson, Mr. Everrett Lewis, Mr. Nesbitt Higgins, Mr. Lionel Charlton and

Mr. Lincoln Taylor, to name a few who had been summoned that evening to confront the level of intolerance parading under the umbrella of the political progressive partisan.

This hurriedly called meeting was to establish a group designed with one objective (i.e.) to advance the interest of Mayaguana island, following the defeat of Mr. Bernard Depuch (Independent), by Mr. T. Joseph. Ford (PLP), Progressive Liberal Party 1968.

At this juncture hope was manifested as a "son of the soil" had been elected to the House of Assembly. The preacher's prophecy had come through.

Islanders were proud and shouted; "All the way. All the time."

T. Joe as he was affectionately called by many was simply a Mayaguana/Inagua child who would look out for the people's interests in parliament. And so it was initially.

Nevertheless, going as far back to World War II, the people in Mayaguana made a shift in political loyalty and voted settlement after settlement for Mr. Bernard Depuch (Independent) instead of Mr. T. Joe Ford (PLP), true story.

Even though Mr. Clayton Taylor had concocted a rationale why the people should vote for "T. Joe", no one took the trashing seriously as his logic was ripe with half-truths and distortions.

The young and older folks who could get out to vote, rallied and a voice were heard loud and clear by the new rulers in Nassau and beyond.

Mr. Bernard Depuch (Independent) who had been elected only a short time earlier, was greatly admired, saw the hand writing on the wall and "forced" retirement was compelled upon him by the residents of Inagua primarily.

Not one person would lie then; Mr. Bernard Depuch (Independent) was a honorable man who acted with some level of integrity, valor and cared greatly about the people of both islands even to this day and time in his old age still, interfaces with many residents.

True true.

As an honorable man who was well loved and continued to show genuine empathy for all people whether P.L.P (Progressive Liberal Party), Independent voters, U.B.P (United Bahamian Party) or the latter day F.N.M (Free National Movement) spoke volumes in the annals of former Members of Parliament, – demeanor and history in the Bahamas.

In the meantime, the debate continues as to why Mayaguanians favored the well known family man called (Dupuches) who they knew best at the time, instead of the sister island residents differing substantially for a man who did have family roots on the island of Inagua.

But again, was it due to the electorate total land size of Inagua or what?

Time never did tell in this instance exactly.

It was apparent at the time, quite singled-handily residents of Inagua elected Mr. T. Joe Ford (PLP) 1968 and later his apparent reaction to the people of Mayaguana as a result of their voting record became evident to many, while the clan associated with Mr. Clayton Taylor aroused his attention and was duly rewarded.

Then again with Mayaguana and Inagua proximity to New Providence island, at this juncture in the British controlled history of the country, the prevailing consensus in the House of Assembly and beyond was "no need" to parcel out an economic stimulus plan, far away from Nassau, the capitol to an island four hundred miles south of any known tourist venue.

It was just how they (i.e.) the members of parliament thought and projected at the time in the Bahamas political and social development.

That was then and so it was, as no forward strategic thinkers dared to craft or structured a plan to birth the growth of light industries, eco-tourism, oil exploration, population growth and housing development outside of New Providence.

Why was that?

"Time will tell…. never forget," the old man would say.

One thing remains clear to this day; T. Joe Ford (PLP) finished the job begun by the renowned family named Depuches, who had been inserted in the country via the colonials past.

T. Joe Ford did get the people new schools, new nurses' clinics, some paved roads between Betsy bay and Pirates Well. That was not all; even the resident commissioner and nurse moved into official and new residences.

Things could not have been better. 1968 true story.

T. Joe Ford was doing what islanders had hoped for from their Member of Parliament. He paid attention to the needs of the people and so it was, as Mr. Clayton Taylor reaped benefits greatly as a result of the Member of Parliament favorable discourse with his clan.

Then a tropical depression clamped down on New Providence island and when it was calm again, the sun shone so brightly with no clouds in sight.

Later in the day, Radio Bahamas ZNS news announced another seismic move by the beloved Honorable Prime Minister

Sir Lynden O. Pindling, had appointed Mr. T. Joe Ford, chairman of another major government operated entity.

To no one surprise. T. Joe Ford was on the up and up and that was for real.

That was just how it had become, while the looting and scattering of the children's dreams and ambitions were fair game at the time for the Chairman of the Board, the Mayaguana Develoment Association (MDA); struggled to offset the thrashing, as it became difficult to maintain as many supporters of Mr. T. Joe Ford abandoned the association and stopped paying membership fees following Mr. T. Joe Ford accession.

No one still knew for sure what had happened. But rumors are not always true, as one thing became crystallized and obvious to people, T. Joe Ford's door and telephone was no longer accessible to many of the constituents of M/I (Mayaguana/Inagua).

The democratically elected Member of Parliament benumbed and reneged on the promises, to be readily available to the voters who had elected him in the first place.

But never give up on the man," an elderly lady from Betsy Bay would always say, as people moved back and forth to the constable residence to use the telephone and get vital mail boat information or just chat about the apparent happenings in town and beyond.

Again this day the beloved constable had made contact with the high command in Abraham's bay, but the commissioner was out fishing with his local confidants even before words had gotten to the constable; gossip was everywhere that the Member of Parliament had taken refuge in New Providence and did not visit Mayaguana hardly anymore.

The Member of Parliament had become noticeably out of sight and residents could no longer reach out and touch him no more.

Though he would show up here and there and someone would always hear where he might have been. True true story.

Then finally word did get from the commissioner's office that he took heart to reveal that T. Joe Ford sounded incoherent and did not give a damn anymore. Something many residents had known for some time. That did not fall well with constituents who voted for him and those who did not vote for him.

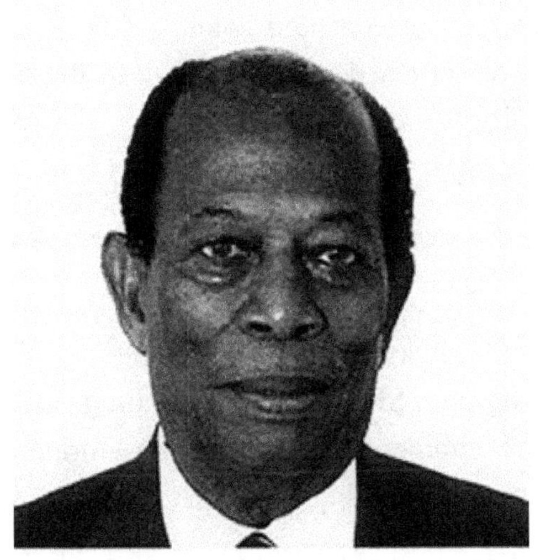

Joseph Ford M.P

Member of Parliament 1968 – 1982

Anyhow who could Mayaguanians turn to?

The mail boat, as slow as it ever was did arrived and were reasonably dependable most of the times when inclement weather did not caused delays.

But the group of civic minded Mayaguanians tried to fill the void and attempted to act as a counter balance to the trifling demeanor displayed by Mr. T. Joe Ford, as the looting and arrest of the beloved children's ambitions and dreams continued.

Who was to give the children a chance?

The bona fide Member of Parliament slipped out of the way and refused to assist the people in any way and to become productive citizens who would live and contribute to the homeland.

Mayaguana and Inagua parents never gave up on their children you know, though the MDA (Mayaguana Development Association), did have a mandate and functioned well to booster the confidence, self esteem and island pride of all who joined even as hope was crushed and dragged into the mud by T. Joe Fords' propensity to berate the promises of the leaders in New Providence.

The children grew up and overcame diversity as the venom heaped on their head by this "son of the soil."

Things are not always what they seem, but with wisdom like Solomon of long ago, Sir Lynden O. Pindling shuffled his cards again and a new cabinet were named with vibrant and confident faces surfacing.

Mr. T. Joe Ford was sidelined to fade in oblivion just before being booted out of the House of Assembly for another "son of the soil" under the banner of the Free National Movement (FNM), who for the most part jiggled politics with a level head, recognizing decorum as mandated by his constituents.

This was clearly not what Mr. Clayton Taylor fought so hard for when campaigning for Mr. T. Joe Ford.

Nevertheless Mr. Vernon Symonette (FNM) did champion the causes for Mayaguana/Inagua people and pleaded for their plight during his tenure in the House of Assembly with marginal success.

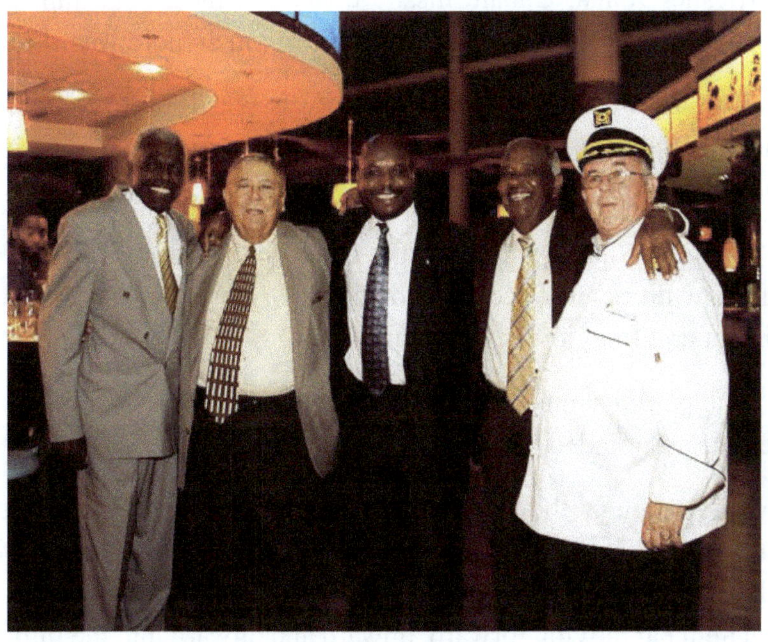

From left to right are: Thomas Robinson, Vernon Symonette, former Speaker of The House, Officer Kenrid Neely, Frank Watson and Chef at Kafe Kalik

Mean while the personalities and characters who did the leg work for the people of Mayaguana succeeded to bring about a dialogue amongst quarters in the community that conveyed the looming threat to the "homeland security" imposed or implied by Nassau that shunned structured economic and civic institutional development in the Family islands.

In retrospect, MDA (Mayaguana Development Association) under the steady eyes of Miss Linda Collie, Miss Roselene Gibson and Mrs. Marie Mckinney, the patron saints of Pirates Well Mayaguana, did mentor the leadership of Mr. Lincoln Taylor (deceased) and also Mr. Lionel Charlton to be proactive and to foment a brotherhood of anchored "indigenous" Mayaguanians who had been witnesses to the turbulence, hurricane Donna, Cuban missile crisis and the rifts within the "house" of Mayaguana and knew well so much more was ahead.

Unlike Mr. Nesbitt Higgins, who was voted into office with much hoopla and cheers? There was great hope and anticipation in his presidency.

Though during his tenure the exodus of anchored Mayaguanians was accelerated, due in part to his disgust for dissent and free flowing dialogue.

The patron saints were never able to tap into his platform as bedlam surrounded his rule.

Even though the partisans of territorial doom and selfish contours triumphed; economic, inter-island commerce, civic advancement, infrastructure development and trade remained a real high bar moving forward, upward and onward into the future.

Time kept slipping into the future was a true; as MDA (Mayaguana Development Association) had many popularly elected presidents and supporting casts who knew a Mayaguana of nine hundred or more inhabitants where emerging enterprises were born even as the exodus to Nassau, Freeport Grand Bahama and beyond where propelled by the surge and flurry for independence from the United Kingdom throughout the Caribbean and African territories.

The Bahamas with a monetary identity on par with the Americans, independence was an ideal escape from the colonial web set by the British.

The Minister That Ran Away From Independent Bahamas

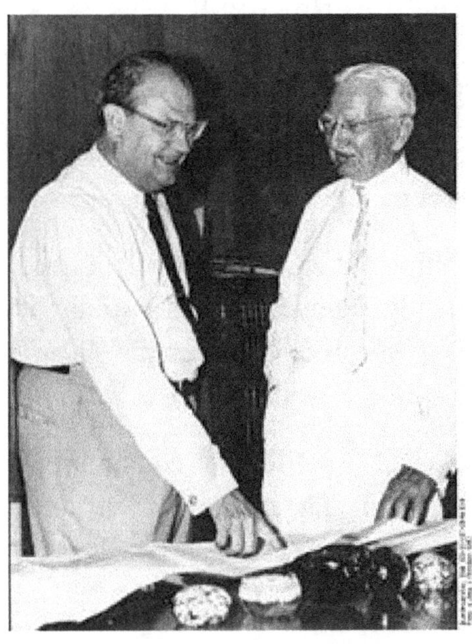

Sir Stafford Sands (left) and Hjalmar Schacht in
October 1962

The smell of Maxwell house coffee was hardly noticed as a
couple of passengers ate in the small kitchen on the starboard side
of the mail boat early in the morning, with partly cloudy skies as
a backdrop and dozens of seagulls hovering overhead. Then the
rain showers started briskly.

But besides the rain the ride so far was not unremarkable as
most persons on board this motor vessel had already emptied
their wallets at a 'favorite' Bay street merchant, for gas, food

supply and other personal effects. This motor vessel was well packed and hurried on as a shuttle crew on a mission.

The rain showers caused the ocean to become fairly choppy. Not one person complained;

They were happily leaving crowded Nassau, going back home to the newly named Family islands. This will take a good two and one half days before anchor will be dropped.

In the distance the Exuma Cay was spotted. They claimed there was a cay for every day of the year.

Anyhow the shipmate was noticed with a hand held transistor radio. He frequently listened to ZNS Radio for the weather report. The radio was really loud, caused we learned later that the engineer did not hear too well in one ear, that was how it was.

Radio Bahamas ZNS spilled out community announcements as many passengers in ear shot of the radio listened to hear perhaps someone named may be mentioned that was known who died at the Princess Margaret Hospital.

But that day there was no ground breaking news or weather alerts bellowing out. The news as it was read; maybe just maybe someone might hear of something that could be very important as the motor vessel plied the waters between the Exuma Cays on the way to the southeastern chain of islands.

Mayaguana (Wednesday) May 25, 1966 with plausible denial and strive acquiescence the United Bahamian Party (UBP) and true many others affluent Bahamians had barrels of pound, shillings and pence ready to be exchanged or returned to the Treasury or Banks for the now legal tender noted to be called dollars and cents.

Sir Stafford Sands, the Bahamian economist turned minister for economic activity was about to pull off another marmot coup;

having watched keenly how the Boers of South Africa initiated draconian types of enactments and laws in over-riding the majority.

The South African had even perpetuated the Westminster type rule of law, created a judicial court of justice and locked up Nelson Mandela then built infrastructures to maintain Soweto style ghettos.

Stafford Sands was avidly adapted to the prevailing radical separatist ideology. No one needed a better platform; he donned the robe of Her Majesty the Queen of England.

He was apartheid driven, so was Johannes Gerhardus Strijdom and Hendrik Frensch Verwoerd, as Pretoria suffered repeated lynching and shootings by the State police machinery of young gifted black and many white men and women who too detested apartheid. Steve Biko cried for help but it was never heard.

At this point the Bahamians had fiercely vomited at the fever of tourism. But to the UBP that was not a problem. They were mostly of European descent and wealthy and knew well the capitalist idiom and practices. Sir Stafford Sands were soon to accomplish something in the annuals history up to this point in the colony's life no one had dared to try.

Sir Stafford Sands mission would be completed with the introduction of the Bahamian dollars ($$$) on par with United States dollars ($$$).

That was excellent not to diminish the earth shaking significance of this event up to this point in the colony's history.

Whether Sir Stafford thought about black majority mile, independence or the Out islanders (as it was called then) Sir Randol Fawkes, Sir Roland Symonette, Granny or anyone for that matter, it was bold.

He thought about fluency, connectivity and of course the legal linkage or parity to the United State Federal Reserve then and in the future.

Hail to the fallen pharaohs who built palaces, gardens and watched his armies defeated. That's nowhere comes the lost tribes of Judah in the Family Islands of M.I.C.A.L (Mayaguana, Inagua, Crooked, Acklins and Long Cay), Long Island, Eleuthera, Exuma, Cat Island and that is not to include the part of Grand Bahama, where Mr. Howard Hughes, the multi millionaire/industrialist American, who employed countless numbers of Bahamians which helped eased the pain of idleness at the time with gainful employment opportunities.

Many U.S. presidents recognized his contribution to medical and industrial research. That was how it seems to be for a long time, but Sir Stafford Sands like then and now; really what was an anonymous path? What too was the decimalization of currency meant?

After World War <u>1</u>, the local central authority supplemented the prewar currencies in circulation. This followed the collapse of the bank of Nassau 1917 - but with increased economic activities on New Providence island, Havana, Port-au-Spain. Port of Prince, Kingston and elsewhere all call for order created the impetus for the establishment of a local tendered) Central Bank notes.

During the occupation of many Caribbean countries above with other Africa based peoples in the Atlantic ocean all U.K. currencies was acceptable up to Nov. 1, 1936; in the colony of the Bahamas, sterling silver was discontinued to be a legal tender for any amount over forty shillings.

May 25, 1966, a new monetary unit was introduced and pegged to the pound sterling at the rate of seven shillings to the dollar. Bahamian notes were issued in multiple units with the currency (Amendment) Act 1967; Sir Stafford Sands the maximum Minister severed all links to the sterling. 1972 the Bahamian dollar predicated by the buttonwood currency dilemma, which led to the floating and devaluation of the U.K. pound.

To be continued as we look at the negligible posture the maximum Minister Sir Stafford Sands dealt with his opponents and the extensive deprivation of native islanders rights to be properly compensated what the colony owed the them as a result of the changes from pound, shilling and pence to the Bahamian dollars (May 25, 1966) never occurred.

SIR RANDOL FAWKES' APPEARED BEFORE THE UNITED NATIONS ON NATIONAL INDEPENDENCE

MR. CHAIRMAN,

DISTINGUISHED REPRESENTATIVES OF THE COMMITTEE ON COLONIALISM

I am here today to secure the encouragement and the concrete assistance of the United Nations in the efforts of the people of the Bahama Islands to prepare themselves for independence.

In this we seek your expert advice and technical assistance in the promotion of the political, economic, and social advancement of the Bahamas that would make a transition from colonialism to freedom less painful than it otherwise would be.

It is our conviction that eternal colonialism in the Bahamas prevents the development of international and economic cooperation, impedes the social, economic and cultural development, and violates the spirit and letter of the Charter of the United Nations. We therefore hope that the United Nations will recognize the indisputable right of the Bahamas to complete freedom and will help us to achieve and exercise our sovereignty and the integrity of our national territory. In faith believing, I relate the following:

On September 1966, your petitioner requested a select committee to take into consideration the advisability of inviting the government of the United Kingdom to convene a constitutional conference with a view to establishing the independence of the Bahama Islands.

Before the speaker could reach the item on the agenda calling for the appointment of select committees, The Premier, Sir Roland Symonette read the following prepared communication: *"I wish to make the following communication to the House in view of the public interest that has been aroused on the question of a constitutional conference on independence. This is a statement that I would have given to the House on Thursday the 25th August if the motion on the agenda for the appointment of a select committee on the subject had been proceeded with on that day:*

As a result of the 1963 Constitutional Conference, the Bahamian Islands now enjoy a constitution which gives the people, through their representatives, virtually full control of their internal governmental affairs.

It has been suggested that because some other countries - perhaps less able to accept full autonomy – have become or are becoming independent, the Bahamas should do the same. The government regards this attitude as misconceived. Independence could be requested, and would no doubt be granted, and this government would be glad to manage the external affairs of the country but the facts must be looked squarely in the face.

Complete independence would impose on our country the financial burden of responsibility for security, defense and external affairs. This burden is at present largely borne by Her Majesty's government, at small cost within the framework of Britain's defense and diplomatic commitments, but it would be extremely expensive, both in money and in manpower for the Bahamas government to take on the task of establishing embassies and high commissions abroad, and of raising and the equipping its own armed forces. Considerable government funds would have to be diverted for these purposes which, in the view of this government, would be much better spent on the progress and development of the Bahama Islands for the good of all the inhabitants. For these reasons the government cannot support proposals for a constitutional conference at the present time."

In due course, the motion was put but was lost by a vote of thirteen to seven. Both Progressive Liberal Bahamian Party and the National Democratic Party supported the motion, but the United Bahamian Party not only denied the courtesy of a select committee, but no member of the party participated in the debate.

Now if we were to examine the statement of the Premier, we will find that his argument against independence is facetious. The premier stated that the Bahamas could not take on the expense of establishing embassies and high commissions abroad but Gentlemen the Bahamas government is now maintaining very highly paid administrative offices in major cities of the world. Some of them in London, Miami, New York, Chicago, Los Angeles, Dallas, St. Louis, Washington, and even in Bonn, Germany.

In many of these offices, Bahamian personnel is either nil or negligible. So the excuse that we cannot maintain an embassy is tenuous indeed.

According to the United Kingdom, we are not Africans, yet "Bahamians" is not a legal term under the constitution, and no one can say with any degree of truth that we are British. As a people we are without history, without culture, and without a national identity. We study British history, British culture, and even British weather, but about ourselves, we have no past – and in colonialism, no future.

Because of the colonial status, the value of the Bahamian dollar is questionable. Should the British pound be devalued, it would have serious consequences on the economy of the Bahamas.

Because of our colonial status, Bahamians pay a penalty in the form of high custom duty for trading with countries other than the British Commonwealth. Our economy is tied to the Western Hemisphere. Indeed everything we eat and wear comes from the Caribbean, North or South America.

It has been suggested that the Bahamas has a democratic constitution based on municipal suffrage – one man, one vote.

Because members in the House of Assembly are not paid, only the rich are financially able to represent their districts – hence membership in the present assembly is composed mainly of the merchants and professional class, but the laboring class has only very limited representation. In the past 200 years, only on two or three occasions have the Out Islands been able to have representation by a person who resides in the Out Islands.

This situation is aggravated by the fact that there is no local government of the Out Islands. These areas are governed only by an appointed commissioner, but there are other elected bodies to assist in the administration. Without more education and greater participation in government, the people will be prepared to master the responsibilities of independence.

We therefore, request that the United Nations take swift action to influence Britain to set a time-table for the eventual independence of the Bahamas and, in the meantime a commission of United Nations experts should be appointed to make a survey of the political, economic and social conditions of the Bahamas with a view to introducing adequate measures that would prepare the Bahamian people to master their own responsibilities.

Who Was Sir Randol Fawkes?

Sir Randol Francis Fawkes often referred to as one of *The Bahamian Fathers*

Two years later the publication of the 1984 Report of a Commission of Inquiry into Drug Trafficking in and through The Bahamas implicated a number of individuals associated with governing party.

Three cabinet members resigned their portfolio responsibilities: Arthur D. Hanna, who had held the post of Deputy Prime Minister and Minister of Finance; George Smith, Minister of Agriculture *of Labor* for the work that he did in establishing the trade union movement in The Bahamas was born on March 20, 1924, Nassau, Bahamas. He was called to the Bahamas Bar in April 1948.

In June 1951, he married the former Jacqueline Rosalie Bethel of West End, Grand Bahamas. There are four children of the union: Francis, Rosalie, Douglas and David.

During the 1950's and 1960's, Sir Randol was in the vanguard of almost every progressive movement: - the *Citizens' Committee* (1949), *The Bahamas Federation* of *Labor* (1955).

After his first election to the House of Assembly in 1956, Sir Randol consistently served on the Select Committees for Labor

Relations and Constitutional Reforms. Association of the Bahamas with the University of the West Indies (UWI) and the Court of Appeal also bear his mark.

In January, 1956, as President of B.F. of L., he led the General Strike, which resulted in major constitutional and labor reforms. In March, 1958 while on a **Lecture** tour of New York City he was cited by the Caribbean League of America and the Abyssinia Baptist Church "in recognition of his outstanding civic contribution to Bahamian life and times." Later in the same year, the National League of Beauty Culturists similarly honored him in Nassau.

In 1961, he successful piloted through the House of Assembly, the Bill which established Labor Day as a public holiday. He was re-elected to the House of Assembly in 1962 and in 1963, Sir Randol represented the Labor Party at the Constitutional Conference in London, England. He was the first representative to raise the question of independence for The Bahamas on the floor of the House of Assembly. In September, 1966, he pleaded the case before the United Nations urging its assistance for the Bahamian people in their stride towards self-determination.

In 1967, his was the decisive vote that broke the 18-18 deadlock between the two major parties: the United Bahamian Party and the Progressive Liberal Party. As a consequence, Majority Rule was then ushered into the country with formation of a PLP-Labor Coalition **government**. From January, 1967 to April, 1968, Sir Randol served as Minister of Labor and Commerce in the first PLP-Labor Government.

In 1972, he returned to the private practice of Law. In recognition of his outstanding contributions to the trade union movement and to the country, knighthood was conferred on Sir Randol by Her Majesty, Queen Elizabeth in 1978. Sir Randol documented his memoirs in a book titled: *The Faith that Moved the Mountain.*

Who was Sir Randol Fawkes

Known to many as one of The Bahamian Founding Fathers

Bahamian Patriot

(March 20th, 1924 - June 15th, 2000)

Randol Fawkes, elder statesman; attorney-at-law; free trade unionist; civil rights activist; sportsman, author and musician, changed the course of Bahamian destiny forever, almost single-handedly.

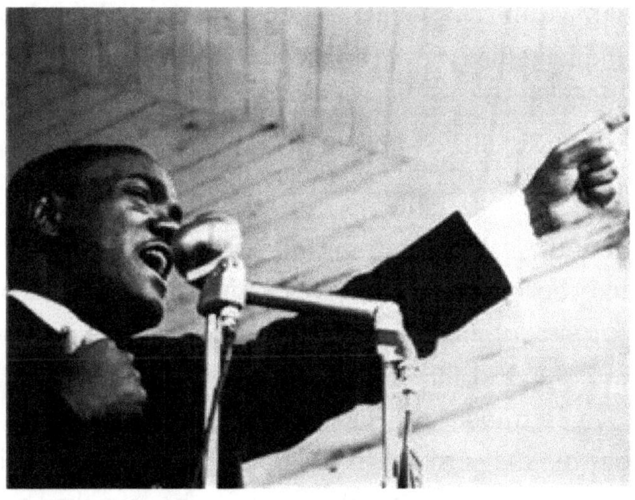

He was born in Nassau on March 20th, 1924 and was the second son of Edward R. Fawkes and Mildred Fawkes. He was educated in the public schools in the Bahamas and in the U.S.A. Three months after his graduation from high school in December1942, Sir Randol's father indentured him to Mr. T. August Toote, a Barrister-at-Law. Afterwards, he was called to the Bahamas' Bar in April 1948. On June 3rd, 1951, Sir Randol married Jacqueline Rosalie nee Bethel of West End, Grand

Bahama. This marriage produced three sons: Francis, Douglas, David and one daughter, Rosalie.

In his struggle for equality for all, this great innovator conceived of many of the social and historical milestones that we as present day Bahamians should not take for granted. As one of the chief architects of majority rule, he was instrumental in bringing into existence the first black government. He is also the recognized father of the Free Trade Union Movement, which is still a formidable force in this country. It is because of Sir Randol Fawkes that a bill was piloted through the House of Assembly thus making Labor Day a paid public holiday.

Because he was a great visionary, many times he anticipated major national developments long before they were recognized or even implemented. For example: the motion for independence; the existence of the Court of Appeal and many other developments are attributable to his farsightedness.

Multi-talented in athletics and the fine arts, he was the President of the Viking Sporting Club. He also showed a flair for music and the visual arts. However, he intuitively recognized God's purpose of his life. His ministry was to the poor and dispossessed and to this end this supreme liberator fulfilled his mission. In Bermuda, he acted in an advisory capacity in the formation of the Progressive Labor Party thus ending an oppressive era of minority rule. In 1999, he launched the trade union movement in the Cayman Islands. For his work at home, he has been honored and officially recognized as the father of Human Rights in the Bahamas.

Perhaps, the greatest legacy he left for this generation was his strength of character. Recognized internationally, he was never spoilt by fame. He never became arrogant or unapproachable. Instead his "mighty meekness" prevailed - and he never lost the common touch. As a highly principled and moral Christian leader, he was tempted by wealth but did not succumb. He was never materialistic, but successfully defended his pension as a matter of principal. His greatest character trait was his willingness to stand up for what he believed in almost life-defying circumstances. This singular quality - which is almost non-existent today - set him apart from most. This seems to be the hallmark of Sir Randol Fawkes one of the greatest foundational leaders of our times.

A Chronology of the accomplishments of this Bahamian Patriot:

1948 - Called to the Bahamas' Bar

1948 - Spearheaded the movement for the existence of the Court of Appeal

1949 - Joined the Citizens' Committee

1951 - Married Jacqueline Rosalie nee Bethel of Grand Bahama

1951 - Founder and secretary of the first commercial bank: The People's Penny Savings Bank

1952 - One of the founding fathers of the Bahamas Amateur Athletic Association (BAAA).

1955 - Founder of the Bahamas Federation of Labor

1955 - One of the founding members of the Progressive Liberal Party

1956 - Elected to the House of Assembly for the Southern District

1956 - Spearheaded the movement for associating the Bahamas with the University of the West Indies

1956 - Served on the house select committee on labor relations and Constitutional reforms

1958 - Played host to the late Dr. Martin Luther King

1958 - As president of the Bahamas Federation of Labor, he led the General strike, resulting in major constitutional and labor Reforms. Later, it paved the downfall of British colonialism in these islands nine (9) years later

1958 - On a lecture tour of New York City, he was recognized by the Caribbean League of America and Abyssinia Baptist Church for Outstanding contributions to Bahamian life and times

1958 - Honored in Nassau by the National League of Beauty Culturalist in Nassau

1959 - In Bermuda he assisted fellow trade unionists in the formation of the Progressive Labor Party as a an alternative to minority rule

1961 - Piloted a bill through the House of Assembly thereby

Establishing Labor Day as a paid public holiday

1961 - Responsible for the resolution for the creation of a Labor Exchange and Old Age Pension Act

1962 - Re-elected to the House of Assembly1963 - Represented the Labor party at a Constitutional Conference in London

1963 - Was one of the first and the strongest proponents for local government in the Bahamas and addressed his concerns at the Constitutional Conference in London 1966 - As one of the first persons on record to advocate national

Independence, he pleaded its cause before the United Nations.

1967 - As an elected Labor leader, broke the deadlock between the United Bahamian Party (UBP) and the Progressive Liberal Party (PLP) by throwing his vote with the P.L.P.

1967 - Became Minister of Labor and Commerce with Copyright Law in his Portfolio in the P.L.P. - Labor Coalition Government.

1967 - Successfully launched the Industrial *****Relations Charter Bahamas in Freeport.

1968 - Represented the Labor Party at the 2nd Constitutional Conference in London

1970 - He was the architect of the November motion of no confidence in the P.L.P. government. This resulted in the dissident eight who formed the basis of the F.N.M. government.

1972 - Listed in *Personalities Caribbean - The International Guide to Who's Who in the West Indies, Bahamas and Bermuda*

1978 - Knight Bachelor conferred by the Queen

1990 - Cited by the Grand Bahama Human Rights Association and the Abaco and the New Providence Associations as the Father of the Human Rights Movement in the Bahamas

1993 - Named man of the year by the Cable Beach Kiwanis Club, New Providence, Bahamas

1997 - Reaches an amicable settlement of his pension case in the Court of Appeal. This resulted in the *Parliamentary Pensions Act 1995* for former parliamentarians and senators; and the *Sir Randol Fawkes Pension Act 1998*

1998 - Received the Silver Jubilee Award in recognition for his outstanding national contribution in the field of Trade Unionism and Labor

1999 - Launched the Trade Union Movement in the Cayman Islands

1999 - Cited as one of the most influential Bahamians of the 20th century in the Tribune's souvenir edition at the turn of the Millennium

1999 - Featured as one of the faces of the century in the Guardian's edition of *Memories - The Turning of a Century*

2000 - Was listed in the Wendell K. Jones Publication: *The 100 Most Outstanding Bahamians of the 20th Century*

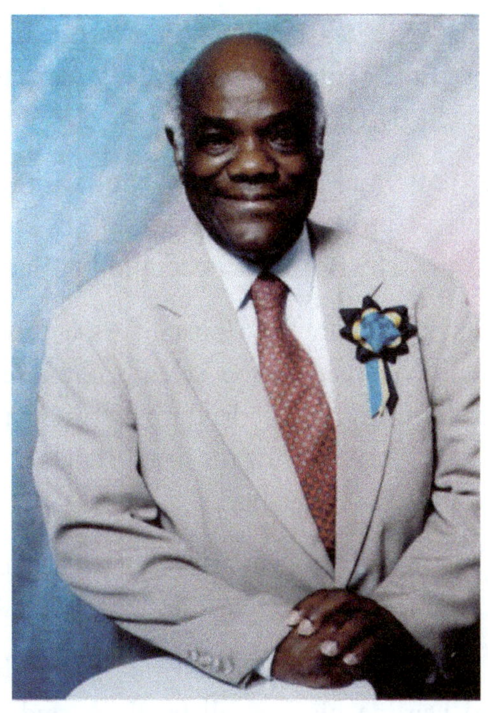

Sir Randol F. Fawkes Bahamian Giant

Sir Randol is often referred to as "The Father of Labor" for the work that he did in establishing the **trade union** movement in The Bahamas. Sir Randol Fawkes, elder statesman, attorney-at-law, free trade unionist, civil rights activist, sportsman, author and musician, changed the course of Bahamian history.

Fawkes was born in Nassau on March 20th, 1924 and was the second son of Edward R. Fawkes and Mildred Fawkes. He was educated in the public schools in The Bahamas and in the U.S.A.

Three months after his graduation from high school in December 1942, Sir Randol's father indentured him to Mr. T. Augustus Toote, a Barrister-at-Law. Afterwards, he was called to the Bahamas Bar in April 1948.

On June 3rd, 1951, Sir Randol married Jacqueline Rosalie nee Bethel of West End, Grand Bahama. This marriage produced three sons: Francis, Douglas, David and one daughter, Rosalie.

During the 1950's and 1960's, Sir Randol was in the vanguard of almost every progressive movement: - the Citizens' Committee (1949), The Bahamas Federation of Labor (1955).

After his first election to the House of Assembly in 1956, Sir Randol consistently served on the Select Committees for Labor Relations and Constitutional Reforms. Association of the Bahamas with the University of the West Indies (UWI) and the Court of Appeal also bear his mark.

In January, 1958, as President of B.F. of L., he led the General Strike, which resulted in major constitutional and labor reforms.

In was in 1957 that the Taxi-Cab Union under the leadership of Sir Clifford Darling blocked all traffic to and from Nassau International Airport in an attempt to halt the Government of the day from granting to the white tour companies "the exclusive franchise to operate transportation services between the new Nassau International Airport and the city."

In 1958, Sir Clifford determined that the efforts of the Taxi Cab Union to satisfactorily resolve the matter were not meeting with success and he contacted Sir Randol who at the time was the President of The Bahamas Federation of Labor which was the umbrella union for the several craft and trade unions that were in existence.

Sir Randol responded with the urgency that the situation required and at a meeting of The Bahamas Federation of Labor presented a motion that stated that the B.F.of L. "should call a General Strike to aid the Taxi Union and to dramatize the plight of all Bahamians for greater dignity and self-respect on the jobsite through decent wages and better working conditions." The motion was unanimously carried.

The situation relating to the Taxi Cab Union in 1958 can best be explained by Sir Randol who as early as 1955 started to use his scholarship, oratorical and writing skills to educate the workers. In 1955, in an article written in the Nassau Herald titled "An Appeal to Reason", he stated, A local union may be able to cope with a small

business firm, but what can it do with a large monopoly? The answer lies in the tying together of all unions into one big Bahamas Federation of Labor. In this way a local union, like the boatmen, the taxicab driver, the electrician, will have the added strength that comes from unity. The Federation will match size for size. A big industrial corporation like the Grand Bahamas Port Authority will meet the Federation, not a tiny union, at the bargaining table."

In March, 1958 while on a lecture tour of New York City, he was cited by the Caribbean League of America and the Abyssinia Baptist Church "in recognition of his outstanding civic contribution to Bahamian life and times." Later in the same year, the National League of Beauty Culturists similarly honored him in Nassau.

Although Labor Day was marked and celebrated in 1956, the first official Labor Day was in 1962. Legislation was necessary to make Labor Day a public holiday and this meant piloting a bill through the House of Assembly.

In 1961, he successful piloted through the House of Assembly, the Bill which established Labor Day as a public holiday. Why did Sir Randol think that it was necessary to have an official Labor Day Holiday? He thought that a day should be set aside and designated as "Labor Day as a fitting memorial to the contributions made by the working people to the progress of the Colony."

When Sir Randol spoke to laboring masses on the first official Labor Day in 1962, he reflected on the first of June morning in 1942 when men and women went on a rampage on Bay Street and demanded better working conditions on the jobsite. Labor Day also was to be a day to commemorate the Burma Road Riot of 1942. "Thanks to them," said Sir Randol, "we now have learned how to substitute the Conference Table for the Riot Act!"

He was re-elected to the House of Assembly in 1962 and in 1963, Sir Randol represented the Labor Party at the Constitutional Conference in London, England.

He was the first representative to raise the question of independence for The Bahamas on the floor of the House of Assembly. In September, 1966, he pleaded the case before the United Nations urging its assistance for the Bahamian people in their stride towards self-determination.

In 1967, his was the decisive vote that broke the 18-18 deadlock between the two major parties: the United Bahamian Party and the Progressive Liberal Party. As a consequence, Majority Rule was then ushered into the country with formation of a PLP-Labor Coalition government. From January, 1967 to April, 1968, Sir Randol served as Minister of Labor and Commerce in the first PLP-Labor Government.

In 1972, he returned to the private practice of Law. In recognition of his outstanding contributions to the trade union movement and to the country, knighthood was conferred on Sir Randol by Her Majesty, Queen Elizabeth in 1978.

Sir Kendal G. L. Isaacs:

The movement that would culminate birth of the Party

The formation of the Free National Movement came to a head on 18 November 1970 when it became clear to eight courageous parliamentary members of the Progressive Liberal Party that their effort to entrench democratic principles in the PLP would fail.

But signs of struggle were evident even earlier. The PLP had come to office for the first time in January 1967. The collapse, three years later, of an agreement between the Government and a consortium of international investors for the upgrading of Bahamas Airways, the national flag carrier, was a red flag indicating to some members of the PLP that all was not well.

Their concern was not only with regard to the impact of the collapse of the agreement on the development of the country's air services but also with the potential damage the collapse could have on investor confidence in the country. Some exclusive international routes granted to Bahamas Airways under the agreement were also given to another airline by the PLP's Civil Aviation Licensing Authority without notice or consultation with the consortium partners.

Some members of the governing party, including ministers, had already been badly shaken in 1969 when Prime Minister Lynden Pindling pressed ahead with the unilateral amendment of the Hawksbill Creek Agreement which set out the terms and conditions for the administration and operation of Freeport by the Grand Bahama Port Authority.

Of primary concern was that the Government's action would halt the development of Freeport which was in no small measure contributing to the full employment levels being enjoyed in the colony at the time. Some of those who had struggled for years to bring the PLP to power were worried about Sir Lynden's increasingly dictatorial style, the decline of collegiality and spreading corruption.

Those in opposition to Sir Lynden's policies and leadership were quickly styled as dissidents and widely vilified by some the party faithful. On the eve of the party's 1970 winter convention a parliamentary member and supporter of Sir Lynden's went on the radio to condemn the dissidents as traitors to the country.

The convention opened in a poisonous atmosphere. Sir Lynden himself targeted the dissidents challenging them to "cut bait or get to hell out of the boat".

Cecil Wallace Whitfield, then Minister of Education, responded in a dramatic speech to the convention and warned the Prime Minister that the same valiant spirits who had helped to bring about the 1967 change could flare up again.

Then he did the unthinkable. He dramatically announced the resignation of his Cabinet post right there in convention and ended his speech with these words: "Free at last! Free at last! My soul is dancing!"

Efforts by Anthony Roberts (later Anglican priest Fr. Roberts) to bring about a reconciliation between the warring groups at an emergency party conclave at the Stokes Thompson Cabana at South Beach failed.

Three of the dissidents, including Sir Cecil, Arthur Foulkes and Maurice Moore, attempted to take their case to PLP supporters in Lewis Yard, Grand Bahama. They were accompanied by Garnet Levarity and others. It was a Sunday afternoon and immediately after the prayers to open the meeting, the dissidents were attacked by a PLP goon squad wielding chairs.

Then, on the evening of the 18 November and early into the next morning the House of Assembly debated a motion of no-confidence in the Prime Minister while outside an angry crowd of Sir Lynden's supporters assembled.

As the debate, raged on for some eleven hours, a counter motion of confidence in the Prime Minister was put, forcing all those in opposition to stand.

Eight parliamentary members of the PLP stood: Cecil V. Wallace Whitfield, Maurice Moore, Arthur A. Foulkes, Warren J. Levarity, James Shepherd, Curtis McMillan, George Thompson and Elwood Donaldson. Dr. McMillan, who was still Minister of Health when Sir Cecil resigned, followed immediately with his own resignation from the Cabinet.

And so the Dissident Eight entered the history books of The Bahamas. Before they got together with others to form the FNM, they referred to themselves as the Free PLP

The crowd outside had grown very hostile towards the Dissidents, especially Sir Cecil, but a police cordon managed to protect them from injury as they made their exit from the House and Parliament Square. The die had been cast.

The 'dissident's were later joined by Kendal Isaacs and Orville Turnquest. Sir Orville had even earlier separated himself from Sir Lynden and Sir Kendal who had done much to help the PLP over the years had also lost confidence in the Prime Minister and his Government.

Shortly thereafter the Dissidents were joined by former members of the disbanded United Bahamian Party and some members of the National Democratic Party. But it was not until

October 1971 that the constitution, first platform (Declaration of Commitment), symbol (the Torch), fanfare (from the Lion in the Winter) and the name of the Free National Movement were settled upon and announced to the Bahamian people.

The new party contested the 1972 general elections as the Free National Movement under Sir Cecil's leadership. Although the FNM polled a total of 19,736 votes, less than 10,000 behind the PLP's 29,628, none of the Dissident Eight was returned in that election.

This notwithstanding, the Dissident Eight had made political history. They are rightly credited with laying the firm foundation for an effective two-party system of government

Growing Pains in a Young Party

By the 1977 general election, dissension within the fledgling FNM had led to a rift. As a result two Opposition parties, the FNM led by Cecil Wallace Whitfield, and the Bahamian Democratic Party led by Kendal Isaacs, faced the incumbent PLP Government led by Sir Lynden and both were soundly defeated. The split cost both parties dearly.

The parties reunited under the banner of the FNM and the leadership of Sir Kendal in time for the 1982 general election and while not victorious won 11 seats in the House of Assembly. The party also made history when its candidate for Yamacraw, attorney Janet Bostwick, became the first female ever elected to the House of Assembly in the Bahamas.

The resignation of Mr. Hanna was purportedly in protest of the inaction by the Government in the face of the allegations. In the case of the other two Ministers, whose names had been implicated by the Report, the resignations served to deflect attention from the scandal encircling the governing party.

Two other Cabinet Ministers, Hubert Ingraham and Perry Christie, were fired from the Cabinet because of their unwillingness to condone or turn a blind eye to corruption in high places. Mr. Ingraham was subsequently expelled from the PLP.

As the 1987 general election drew near popular support for the FNM appeared to reach unprecedented levels and the party had high expectations of winning the election. That did not happen. The FNM won only seventeen of the forty nine seats in the House of Assembly. However the two Cabinet Ministers fired by Sir Lynden were successfully re-elected to the House as Independents. This was a very different scenario.

Kendal Isaacs resigned as Party Leader following the 1987 general election loss and Cecil Wallace Whitfield once again assumed leadership. Orville Turnquest was Deputy Leader. Shortly thereafter, Sir Cecil's health began to fail.

Subsequently, Sir Cecil and others in the FNM began a campaign to attract Hubert Ingraham to the FNM. Mr. Ingraham joined the FNM in April 1990 and was made Parliamentary Leader of the Party. When Sir Cecil passed away the next month, the FNM's Central Council unanimously elected Mr. Ingraham Party Leader.

Mr. Ingraham led the FNM in a successful by-election to fill the Marco City (Grand Bahama) seat left vacant by Sir Cecil's death. He then set about rebuilding the party in preparation for the 1992 general election.

Following a hotly contested election season the FNM swept the August 1992 general election, winning thirty two of the forty nine seats to become the Government of the Bahamas. Sir Cecil's prophetic warning to Sir Lynden in 1970 had finally come to pass.

As promised during the election campaign, the FNM Government immediately reduced the salary of parliamentarians, reduced the number of seats in the House of Assembly from forty nine to forty, broke the Government's monopoly of the airwaves by introducing private radio to The Bahamas for the first time, completed the electrification of all the Family Islands, commenced an ambitious programme to expand the Government-operated school plant thereby reducing class size, and introduced elected local government in the Family Islands.

Five years later, in 1997, in a strong vote of confidence in FNM administration, the party was returned to office with thirty four of the forty seats. Later that year, in the by-election to fill the seat vacated by the retiring PLP Leader and former Prime Minister Sir Lynden Pindling, the FNM increased their majority to thirty-five

During its second term in office FNM policies succeeded in bringing the unemployment rate to a single digit, a level not experienced since the mid-1960s, and in two consecutive years the FNM government produced a balanced recurrent budget. The programme to construct new community health care facilities in partnership with the National Insurance Board was further advanced during the second term, as were the school expansion and the road reconstruction and upgrade programmes, both commenced during the party's first term in office.

Haing committed not to seek more than two consecutive terms in office as Prime 1 Minister, Mr. Ingraham signaled that he would not seek re-election as Leader of the FNM at the Party's next convention and would not serve as Party Leader following the 2002 general election.

Sir Kendal G. L. Isaacs' and His Political Party FNM.

Election Loss and Re-evaluation

The campaign to succeed Mr. Ingraham became acrimonious as four Cabinet Ministers made known their interest in succeeding to the post of Party Leader.

In September 2001, the FNM called a Special Convention to elect a Leader-Designate and Deputy Leader-Designate. The hotly contested election was won by Tommy Turnquest, then Minister of Tourism, who became Leader-Designate. Education Minister, Dion Foulkes was chosen as Deputy Leader-Designate.

The fallout from the Party elections revealed that fissures in the Party that had been submerged during two consecutive election victories at the polls were still present. The hard won united front present in 1992 and 1997 was no longer present as the FNM went into the 2002 general election. Two former cabinet ministers ran as independents.

Discord in the party combined with historic low voter turnout brought dramatic results. The Free National Movement was swept from office, winning only seven of forty seats, and only a single seat in New Providence.

Party Leader Tommy Turnquest lost his seat but was convinced to remain on as Leader of the party. He was appointed by the Governor-General as a Member of the Senate, and leads the Opposition's business in that Chamber.

Mr. Alvin Smith, the FNM Member of Parliament for North Eleuthera, was chosen as Leader of the Opposition in the House of Assembly.

The FNM entered upon a three-year period of self-examination and rebuilding of the party's base under the leadership of Tommy Turnquest. Then, in an initiative led by the FNM's Parliamentary Group, the FNM wider membership succeeded in convincing Hubert Ingraham to return to active leadership of the party.

Mr. Ingraham agreed to have his name entered into nomination for the post of Leader at the Party's Convention in October 2005 and was easily elected. Brent Symonette, the FNM MP for Montagu, was elected Deputy Leader.

With a tried and tested leader at its helm and a reinvigorated party base, the FNM is preparing to face its old political foe at the polls in a general election which must be called before the end of May 2007.

After 35 years of existence the FNM remains committed to the principles which prompted its birth as a party: a deep and abiding respect for democratic principles, a commitment to integrity and honesty in office, a pledge to transparency and accountability in government, and a promise to govern in the people's name for the benefit of all Bahamians.

(Excerpts from the Free National Movement historical archives)

(For more details contact Free National Movement – Nassau Bahamas).

Who was the United Bahamian Party? (UBP)

Bahamas Political Party History

For decades, the white-dominated United Bahamian Party (UBP) ruled The Bahamas, then a dependency of the United Kingdom, while a group of influential white merchants, known as the "Bay Street Boys," dominated the local economy.

In 1953, Bahamians dissatisfied with UBP rule formed the opposition Progressive Liberal Party (PLP). Under the leadership of Lynden Pindling, the PLP won control of the government in 1967 and led The Bahamas to full independence in 1973. Pindling is credited in spurring the development of international banking and investment management as a major industry and most importantly for fighting for equal rights for all Bahamians.

In 1971, dissatisfied with the PLP party a coalition of PLP members and former UBP members formed the Free National Movement (FNM).

In the 1980s, Pindling and members of his party were *accused* of corruption and accepting bribes from drug traffickers. Those allegations and a depressed economy (caused by his government's xenophobic policies towards foreigners--the lifeblood of the country's economy) contributed to his party's defeat in 1992 by the Free National Movement (FNM) which promised freer markets and less government intervention in personal affairs.

Former PLP cabinet minister and Member of Parliament Hubert Ingraham became leader of the FNM in 1990.

Under Ingraham's leadership, and the Bahamian people's dissatisfaction with the PLP's ruining of the Bahamian economy, the FNM won control of the government from the PLP in the August 1992 general elections. Winning again in March 1997, the ruling FNM controlled 35 seats in the House of Assembly, while the PLP controls four seats and serves as the official opposition.

The principal focus of the then Ingraham administration has been economic development and job creation. Many of his government's policies are aimed at improving the image of The Bahamas and making it an attractive place for foreigners to invest by adopting more free-market oriented policies, operating under a rule of law.

Other challenges are to privatize The Bahamas' costly, inefficient national corporations, such as the Batelco the state's inefficient, overpriced (by several 100%) phone company, provide job retraining for hundreds of workers who will be affected by the change, and to continue creating jobs for new entries in the employment market.

In May 2002, the Progressive Liberal Party (PLP), led by veteran politician Perry Christie, was returned to office, replacing the Free National Movement (FNM), which had run the government for the past decade.

The FNM, led by Senator Tommy Turnquest after Prime Minister Hubert Ingraham voluntarily relinquished control of the party, was beaten badly and is in some disarray. In 2006, the PLP holds twenty-nine seats in the forty-member House of Assembly, while the FNM holds seven and the remaining four are controlled by independents.

The PLP government will not have to call new elections until 2007, which are held every 5 years.

The Honorable. Carlton Francis

BAHAMIAN EDUCATORS

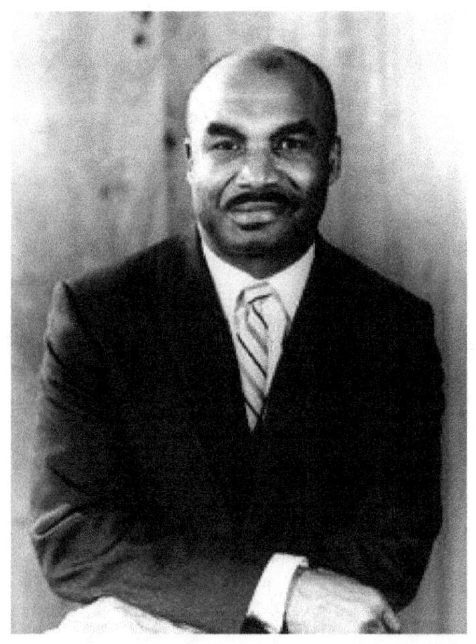

Rev. Carlton Francis, 1919 - Department of Archives.

"There is a path for honorable men to follow when they find they can no longer follow their leader." The Rev. Carlton Francis

Rev. Carlton Francis was born in Miami, Florida in 1919. He was educated at the Government High School, Nassau. He received further education at St. Andrew's University in Scotland, Edinburgh University and the University of the West Indies.

Mr. Francis had a long career in the field of Education. From 1955 - 1956 he was head teacher and principal of the Southern Senior, Western Senior and Eastern Senior Schools. He also taught at Jordan Memorial, Prince Williams High, The Bahamas Teacher's Training College and Queen's College.

Some Bright Spots in Truth (Bahamas) in Brief:

The Bahama Islands were happened upon during Christopher Columbus's first voyage and settled by Spaniards the first decades of the sixteenth century. The islands had no real usefulness to Spain other than used as a staging ground for other expeditions throughout the Caribbean, but the role was greatly enhanced with the American Civil War imploding 1861 – 1865 and later the rum running era through North America and the Caribbean hastened the plight.

The discovery of the so-called "New World" was one link in a chain of events that started four hundred years before as the Crusades began and with this monopoly, the capture of the city of Constantinople by the Turks in 1453, the Atlantic ocean countries, notably Portugal, Spain, France, England and Holland searched for other routes to India and China.

With sailors leading they headed in all directions looking for routes to Asia so as to bypass Italian cities and the Turkish city of Constantinople, now Istanbul.

As result, men like Columbus, John Cabrot, Pedro Cabrol, Ferdinand Magellan, Amerigo Vespucci, Hernando Cortez, Francisco Picarro, Vasco de Balboa, Giovanni de Verranzano and Juan Ponce de Leon, not only did they find an all water route to the east, they also found a vast new hemisphere lying between Europe and Asia.

Spain became the leading nation in launching expeditions for exploration and colonialization.

However, England, with control of most of now United States of America, in 1640 gave patent (exclusive rights) to the Lord Proprietors based in the Carolinas, the chain of islands known now as the Commonwealth of the Bahamas.

These wealthy Lords as they were called notably named Christopher, Duke of Albernale, William, Earl of Craven, John Lord Berkeley, Anthony Lord Ashley, Sir George Carleret and Peter Colleton.

Within forty years the Lord Proprietors plotted fortune on a perpetual basis through various seagoing ventures.

Never did the Lord Proprietors know what to expect, with the English occupation of Havana, Cuba 1762 -63, new opportunities for trade emerged with New Providence's linkages to Britain, North America and the English speaking Caribbean contributed to the influx of new political ideas, customs and forms of organizations.

Nor was the Spanish Acquisition all the Lord Proprietors had to worry about. The French was active in Hispaniola and had other ambitions, the islands of the Bahamas had little defense, the authorities in New Providence called and pleaded for a garrison and a frigate.

The Bahamas have always been extremely vulnerable to foreign attacks since 1492, but remained at the mercy of Mary Read, Anne Bonney the "lady" pirates with Calico Jack Rackham and Stede Bonnet, the Barbadian.

New Providence with Nassau as a base saw more carnage continued by Blackbeard, who sailed toward the southeast searching the ocean for Jamaica and Barbados, later Benjamin Hornigold and Charles Vane plied the waters and more pillage continued.

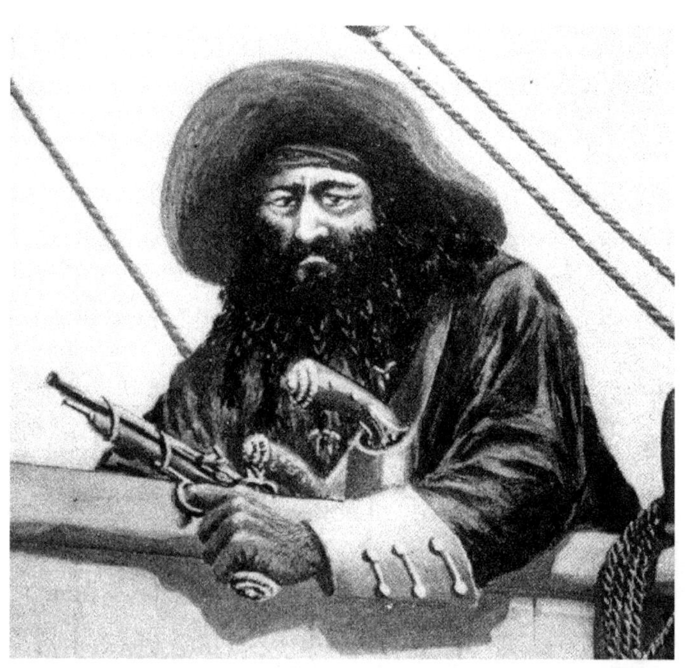

Blackbeard

A number of pirate leaders had twenty to fifty men working and were acquainted with the inhabitants of the islands and fear was echoed in the writings of Graves, that the pirates were on the verge of taking control of the islands.

The Lord Proprietors were known to be neglectful and most unscrupulous, they had granted Hog island, now Paradise island to Trott for about $80.00, all of Exuma and the forest rights to the braziletto trees to Henry Palmer.

The New Providence treasurer was paid less than $23.00 for Paradise island aka Hog island and all of the species of trees on Exuma.

The salt of the Bahamas alone made retention worthwhile. This commodity was vital for provisioning ships and for the fishing industries of Newfoundland and New England.

The Lord Proprietors had little or no interests in the islands as a whole; they treasured certain islands namely New Providence, Exuma and Hog islands.

John Graves wrote to the Crown begging that the islands be placed under English control instead of the Lord Proprietors, but cried out weeping when he noticed that the Crown had little or no interest in the islands of the southern and central Bahamas.

In 1706 John Graves claimed the total population of the Bahamas at about 400- 500 families scattered over two hundred miles; namely Cat, Exuma, and Eleuthera and Harbor islands amongst a few others. No inhabitants had yet clustered on the island of Mayaguana, while the settlers in New Providence island lived in small huts and were always ready to fight off the assaults of Blackbeard, Hornigold, Ann Bonney, Mary Read, Calico Jack Rackham and Steve Bonnet slaughtering as they roamed the bushes and waterway.

> – I left the island 27 families and at least four hundred to – five hundred people scattered, but in a little time they will be worse than the wild Indians and at the very best many are ready, willing and able to help and trade with the Pirates," lamented John Graves.

Due to the scanty materials in the island there was no government or semblance of one anywhere in the Bahamian archipelago. By the end of the war of Spanish succession, the pirates were in total control of the islands.

In 1708 John Graves addressed a Memorial to the Proprietors and the Commissioners of Customs, the only known copy can be viewed at the Nassau public library, he echoed these sentiments; "If the Spanish take possession which I hear they said they could, all trade from North America to Jamaica will be hazardous and from Carolina to Jamaica may be obstructed, while trade may be forced to move between several of the islands to reach Jamaica." John Graves was deeply distressed and disliked the Lord Proprietors.

Only two days from Havana, Cuba, the harbor of Nassau is still a valuable prize. By 1713, several hundred pirates were active in the islands of the Bahamas with various activities and hardly a true government.

In 1714 Gov. Pulleine of Bermuda cried that 200 families were in constant fear and anarchy had settled in.

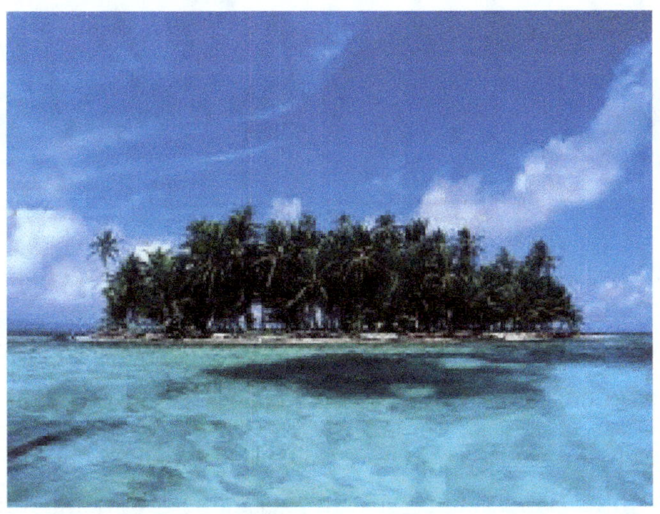

(coconut trees surrounded the ocean)

Three sets of pirates ruled. Cockran controlled Harbor island, where he wed the daughter of on Thompson, but Barrow and Hornigold controlled New Providence and styled themselves governors.

By then, Thomas Walker was doing his best to assist the authority of the Crown. He was Judge of the Admiralty Court by William III, but his appointment was never confirmed by Queen Anne. The islands of the Bahamas were always vulnerable to attacks as raid continued regularly from Havana, Cuba and Thomas Walker fled to Habakoe (aka) Abaco as it is now called.

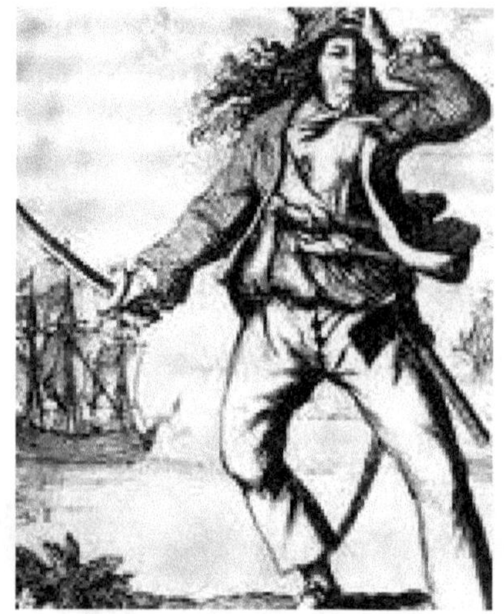

Mary Read

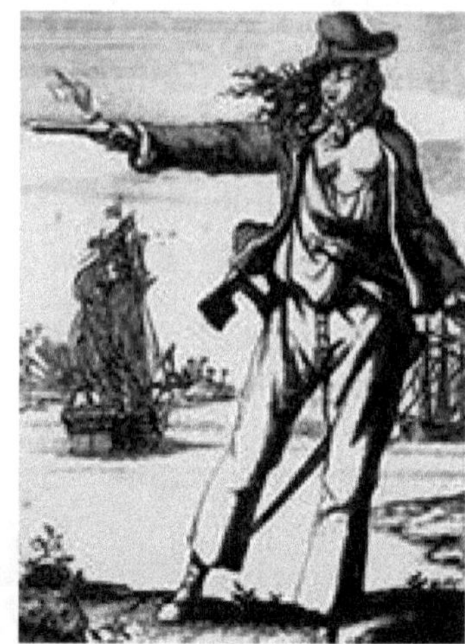

Anne Bonney

Mary Read and Anne Bonney, the "lady" pirates coupled up with "Calico" Jack Rackham and Stede Bonnet, the Barbadian planter pirates. But the leaders had been Benjamin Hornigold, Charles Vane and Edward Teach – aka - Blackbeard.

Blackbeard pretty much controlled the islands. He is a synonym for Bahamian piracy. In Nassau he is remembered by a Tavern and a well in Pirates Well, Mayaguana. He alone is best known of all historical personalities in Bahamian history.

While the history of Blackbeard is grossly exaggerated, simply to add humor to his legacy. The hair of his beard was always in plaits. He wore six pistols in his belt and firing slow matches in his hat band.

Blackbeard - aka -Edward Teach – much of his cruelties are legendary. A physical giant believed to have had fourteen wives. He was captured in or around 1718 while licking his wounds in a fight.

His drinking of liquor was never matched then or since. One favorite story is known at the climax of a drinking spree, where he'd placed burning sulphur, closed the hatch and shouted, "We have made our own hell. Let us see who is closest to the devil, by staying the longest in it."

The real Teach was considerably smaller than the man in the legend. A Bristol seaman, he served as a privateer during Queen Ann's war. After 1713, he joined up with Hornigold and finally gained a ship of his owned by 1716. He captured merchants and loaded his ship with guns and cut-throats, later naming his ship ironically, Queen Anne's Revenge.

His career lasted only two years and made much havoc and trouble while amassing great wealth and fortune. There were many pirates and only the ruthless survived.

"Rum all out, men are now sober, a damned confusion with us. Rogues are plotting great talk of separation – so I looked sharped for a prize. Took one with a great load of liquor aboard, so it kept the men hot, then all things went well again, "so shouted Blackbeard.

1717, Board of trade, Captain Mathew Muscon, mentioned Blackbeard alongside four other pirate captains, (Hornigold, Jennings, Burgess and White) who used New Providence as a base, with over 360 men. The following years, Gov. Robert Johnson of South Carolina regarded Blackbeard as the main threat to disorder and chaos in the islands of the Bahamas.

Gov. Robert Johnson continued; "The unspeakable calamity this poor province suffers from pirates obliges me to inform yo' Lordships of it. In order that His Majesty may know and be indeed to afford us the assistance of a frigate or two to cruise hereabouts upon them for we are continually alarmed and our ships are taken and then our trade."

Blackbeard is character to avert, which was marked by brutality, murder and tragic plunder.

True, he left a name for himself even to this day, but we ought to know some veracity as it is written of the man and boldly began to thrust the new "MICAL" pride.

This is a day to gallantly ferment and forge a new thought and pursue a continual historical growth and development and make known to the globe the stories of our people's struggle, progress and involvement in a new Bahamas government against this backdrop.

Not a single person is known to have lived on the island of Mayaguana before 1812. Later sailors settled with their families alongside Abraham's bay, Pirates Well and Betsy bay from Turks and Caicos islands, farmed the land, growing cattle, hunting ducks, fished for food and worshiped and praised the Creator for the serenity of Mayaguana.

1812 – 1848, the petrified inhabitants of Turks and Caicos island petitioned the Secretary of State, seeking help from the so-called Crown in London, but was never assisted in any way recorded, creating an exodus as residents sojourned to the islands close to the Turks Caicos, seeking freedom of religion , assembly and prosperity from the bondage of the colonial Barons.

Much from such efforts were noted when working together. Perhaps today the dominate authority in the capitol may find a way for (FAF) "Fairness Appropriation of Funds) for MICAL and hasten a stimulus package with the Nassau/Freeport Basin (NFB).

How much of all Capital Expenditure is assigned for Family Island development?

Examples are clear

Capital Expenditure 2013/14 vs. 2014/15

FY2014 FY2015 Variance Growth

Ministry of Finance $ 115,600,000 $ 120,800,000 $ 5,200,000 4.5%

Ministry of Works and Urban Development $ 111,979,248 $ 125,934,120 $ 13,954,872 12.5%

Royal Bahamas Defence Force $ 28,124,413 $ 39,250,000 $ 11,125,587 39.6%

Ministry of Education, Science and Technology $ 16,378,600 $ 24,919,136 $ 8,540,536 52.1%

Customs Department $ 4,213,000 $ 3,700,000 $ (513,000) -12.2%

RoyalBahamas Police Force $ 4,190,000 $ 1,855,000 $ (2,335,000) -55.7%

Heads not Repeated $ 4,000,000 $ - $ (4,000,000) -100.0%

Ministry of Agriculture, Marine Resources &Local

Government

$ 2,935,000 $ 1,680,000 $ (1,255,000) -42.8%

Ministry of Youth, Sports and Culture $ 2,635,000 $ 8,430,000 $ 5,795,000 219.9%

Department of Civil Aviation $ 2,200,000 $ 1,975,000 $ (225,000) -10.2%

Ministry of Health $ 1,035,000 $ 500,000 $ (535,000) -51.7%

Department of Housing $ 750,000 $ 1,200,000 $ 450,000 60.0%

Prisons Department $ 650,000 $ 650,000 $ - 0.0%

Ministry of NationalSecurity $ 500,000 $ 500,000 $ - 0.0%

Total Capital Expenditure $ 295,190,261 $ 331,393,256 $ 36,202,995 12.3%

My National Heroes
Sir Lynden O. Pindling, the true Father of the Bahamas

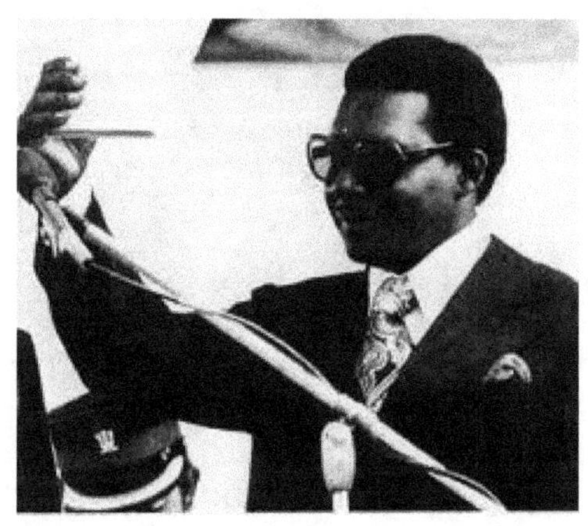

Sir Lynden Oscar Pindling KCMG, OM, JP (22 March 1930 – 26 August 2000), The only true "Father of the Nation" of the Bahamas

Sir Clifford Darling

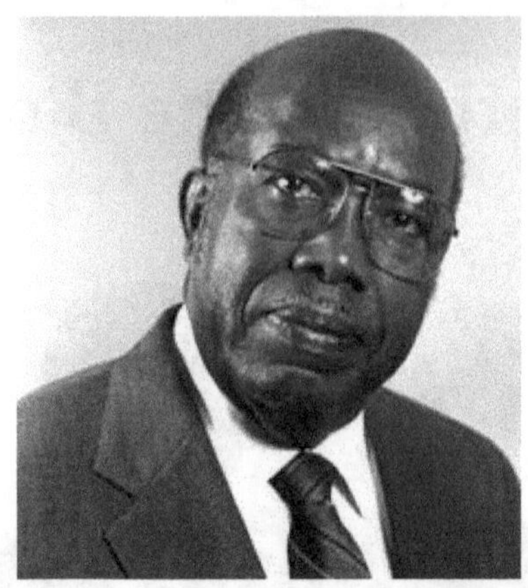

HIS EXCELLENCY SIR CLIFFORD DARLING,
KT., J.P.
Governor-General of The Commonwealth of The
Bahamas
1992 – 1995

His Excellency Sir Clifford Darling, Kt., J.P., is the fourth Bahamian-born Governor General of the Commonwealth of The Bahamas.

Sir Clifford was sworn in at Government House on January 2, 1992, by Chief Justice Joaquim Gonsalves-Sabola, succeeding His Excellency Sir Henry Taylor, Kt., J.P., who retired on January 1.

Cecil Wallace-Whitfield

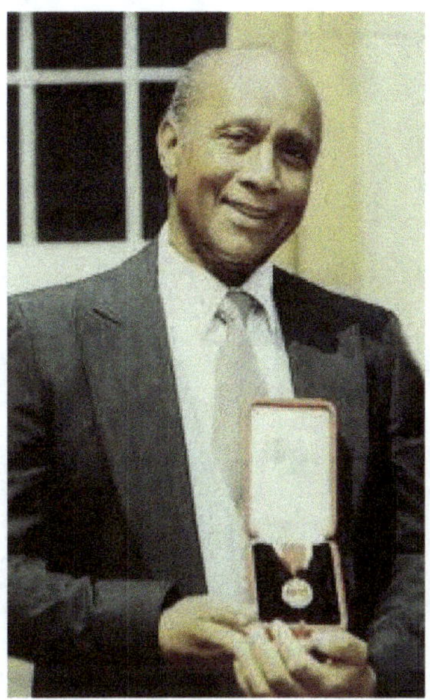

Born: 20-Mar-1930

Birthplace: Nassau

Died: 09-May-1990

Executive summary: Founder of the FNM. Leader of the political movement in 1970, when eight parliamentary members left the PLP and became known as "The Dissident Eight".

These men formed the Free-PLP but subsequently changed the party's name to the Free National Movement (FNM) later that year.

Sir Milo Butler (1906 – 1979)

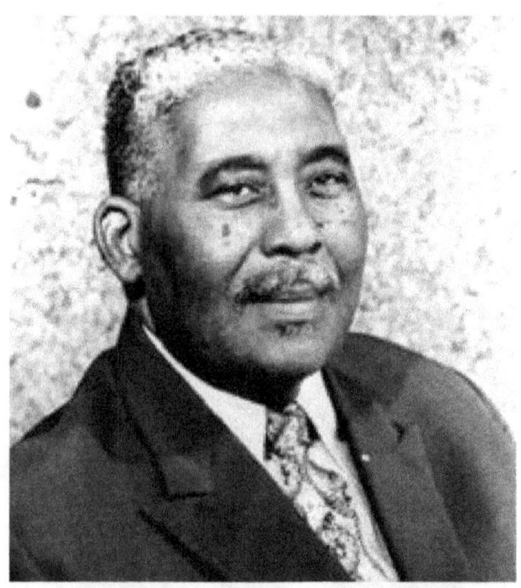

Sir Milo Butler member of the House of Assembly (Parliament) and the first governor-general of the Bahamas.

In the House chamber Butler called for the purging of white rule in the country. Butler's provocative social action was unsettling; it abraded the social order. He had also challenged the social order symbolically, because the upper stratum of British society in general, and the codified venue of the House in particular, prided itself on a high degree of "decorum."

Bahamas Colonial Mansion

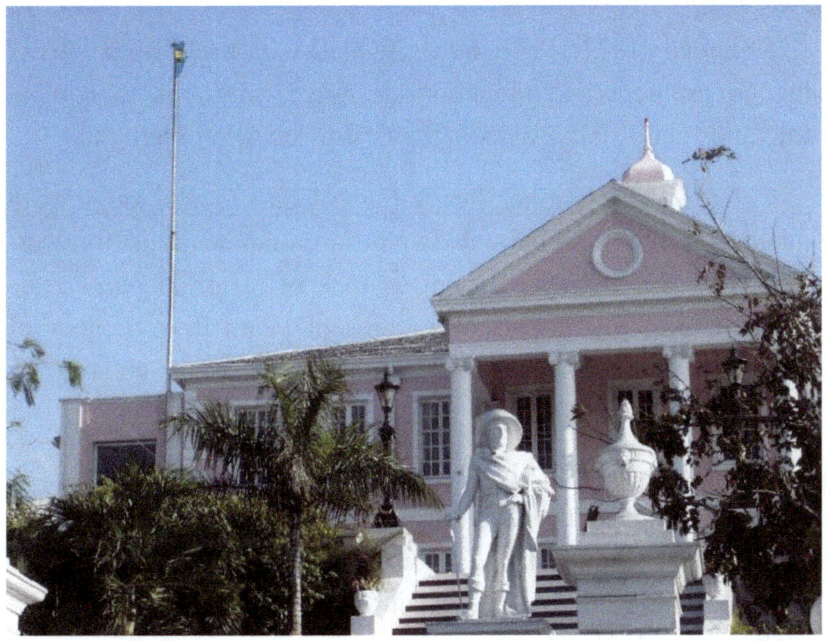

Looking To Track Crime:

Looking to track "quality of life crimes", namely in New Providence Bahamas ever likely?

I believe the blitz may be associated with the confusing way the government and the court designed programs to combat tolerance and illicit usages in the first place as problematic.

Police Commissioner has yet to pledge to get tough with quality of life offenders. Now, how could he hope for trust alongside the history of rising crimes of terror in part to the invasive drug incursions of the recent years in a number of localities namely New Providence and other urban cells in the northern Bahamas.

In what may be a first crime initiative since Sept 11,2012, Police Commissioner could begin in the climate of political intrigue and electioneering, crack down on so called nuisance crimes as does the department with more serious local ordinance violations and infractions.

I believe a map of quality of life hot spots around the islands could began to track trends of shootings, robberies, burglaries, car theft, crimes associated with gambling, vehicular homicides and domestic violence should be known to all key players in this endeavor.

Furthermore, to garner reasonable results, publicizing a crime hot line, available nationwide as a totally free telephone number, 24/7, could very well loan to community participation in tackling the menace.

Crime has reached a level unacceptable to rational civil order in New Providence as District police Commanders has yet to be held accountable for how they deal with crime in these assigned area(s).

Community tolerance of crime in Blue Hill, Fox Hill, Yellow Elder, and Bamboo town, Kennedy Subdivision, Bain Town, Coconut Grove and Carmichael could be lowered and a dramatic upsurge in residents' awareness levels increase while acceptance of sober social norms returning to each community.

Basically how members of the community began to deal with one another should be a strategy of great concern to the Commanders.

No doubt aggressive street hookers, peddlers, panhandlers may be notorious throughout town, while loud and excessive rowdiness, "wilding-out" and cultural music, irate citizens have become less likely to seek police assistance, due in part to residents overall confidence in the police machinery has faded over the years.

Police Commissioner has yet to pledge a tough and reasonable community based police approach to crime stoppage and prevention with legitimacy and resolution to bring down the high blitz of quality of life crime and fear in the metro Nassau area.

Murder, manslaughter, vehicular homicides, cargo theft, domestic violence and widen drug incursions throughout central Nassau is a known fact, statistics has been alarmingly high for twelve years, compared to cities with population of less than 500,000 people.

Police Commissioner and the Prime Minister have yet to repeatedly stress whether strict enforcement would be forthcoming and announces their pledged commitment to solving the island-wide disorder.

I seriously believe quality of life crimes should become more a targeted plan for crime reduction and public concern in 2015 - 2018.

Community tolerance of crime in Blue Hill, Fox hill, Yellow Elder, Bamboo town, Carmichael, Fort Charlotte,

Bain town and much of the known over the hill areas could be lowered and a dramatic upsurge in residents' awareness level increase with the acceptance of sober social norms resurgence.

Basically how members of the community began to deal with one another should be a matter of great concern to community leaders and police commanders who may be cognitive of issues prevalent in the above areas.

No doubt, aggressive street hookers, peddlers, panhandlers may be notorious throughout town, as loud music and excessive rowdiness, "wilding-out" and heavy drinking of intoxicating beverages contributes substantially to the lowering of public confidence in the police response to the problems.

Meanwhile police tactics known to residents who have had to deal with questionable ways some members of the force have dealt with the drug trade have gone un-noticed by the authorities for over twenty five years.

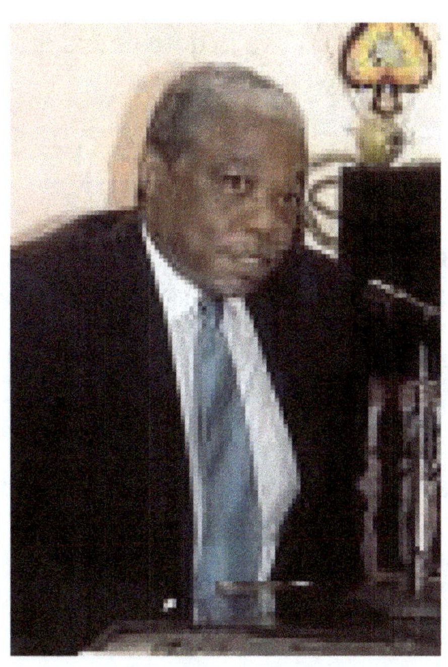

Hon. Bernard Nottage
Minister of National Security (2015 – 2017) Bahamas.

Meanwhile some have begun to question whether the named "national security" minister is really up to the task since the public demeanor continues to be elitist and suggests one that is not inclusive of others who for no reason have not been given an opportunity to serve.

More people are out of work in the Bahamas than has been in a century, while many people look for work some are resorting to crime as a means to an end.

However, the upward trend is mystifying and confusing criminologists who says Bahamians are normally quiet and peaceful people but with the influx of cocaine and the continued usage of crack and the heavy drinking associated with the same it is believed more programs to discourage drugs use would help as well as an orchestrated planned economic development will only help to lift many who live in despair and are fed up with the government inattention to their plight.

(Crime and Punishment) will continue to be viewed and watched as time slips into the future).

COMMISSIONER ELLISON E. GREENSLADE MEETS THE PRESS 20TH JANUARY 2015 @ 11:00AM

PAUL FARQUHARSON CONFERENCE CENTER POLICE HEADQUARTERS NASSAU

Serious Crimes New Providence Bahamas

One hundred and eight (108) murders were recorded in New Providence in 2014 as compared to one hundred and twelve Murders (112) recorded in 2013. This represents a 4% decrease in murders in New Providence for 2014 when compared to 2013.

Almost every category of serious crime in New Providence showed double digit decreases in 2014!

The figure s are as follows:

! Murder down   4%

! Attempted Murder up   67%

! Manslaughter down   33%

! Rape down   26%

! Attemptedrape down   40%

! Unlawful Sexual Intercourse
   down   31%

! Armed Robbery down   9%

! Robbery down   2%

! Burglary down   21%

! Housebreaking down   22%

! Shop breaking down   14%

! Stealing dow   22%

! Stealing from Vehicle down   16%

! Stolen Vehicle down   24%

Illegal Firearms and Ammunition Seizures

In 2014 police officers were able to take four hundred (400) illegal

Firearms off the streets of The Bahamas (predominantly (New Providence). This number included: 219 pistols, 41 revolvers, 33rifles, 69 shotguns, 6 high powered firearms, 4 other types of weapons, and 21 imitation firearms. Of the total amount of weapons seized, The Pistol (55%) still remains the weapon of choice by offenders with the shotgun (17%), and Revolver (10%) following. In addition to the confiscated weapons, seven (7) firearms surrendered by Licensees due to the increase in firearms licensing fees.

Ammunition Confiscated and Surrendered

There were seven thousand five hundred forty-five (7,545) rounds Of ammunition seized in 2014.The amounts and caliber of ammunition seized are as follows:

! (662)   22 caliber,

! (498)   223 caliber,

! (62)   25 caliber,

! (31)   32 caliber,

! (407)   357 caliber,

! (343)   .38 Special caliber,

! (321)   380 caliber

! (1154)   40 caliber,

! (17)   44 caliber,

! (680)   45 caliber,

! (47)   556 caliber,

! (275)   7.62 caliber,

! (1641)   9mm caliber,

! (1058)   12 gauge shells, and

! (150)   20 gauge shells.

A total of two hundred ninety-nine (299) persons were arrested for possessing illegal firearms and for firearms related matters. Two hundred fifty were adult males, thirteen juvenile males, thirty-three adult females and three juvenile females. Of this total, 62% of the suspects were charged and placed before the criminal courts.

The records indicated accurately that the Royal Bahamas Police Department under the Leadership of the current Commissioner has demonstrated a keen willingness to deal with the high level of vices and crime in the islands of the Bahamas and he must be given praise for the efforts by the local Policemen on the beat.

The Bahamas Police Department must be congratulated and praised.

Sir Authur Foulkes

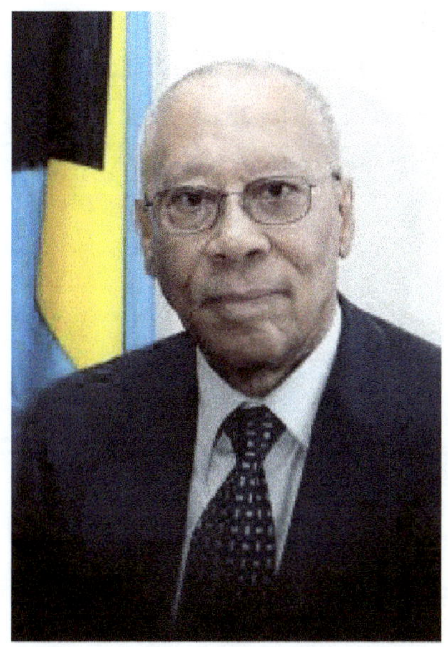

His Excellency Sir Arthur Alexander Foulkes is the eighth Bahamian Governor-General of the Commonwealth of The Bahamas. Sir Arthur was sworn in on April 14, 2010, upon the retirement of Governor-General the Honourable Arthur Dion Hanna.

In recognition of his new status, Her Majesty Queen Elizabeth II elevated Sir Arthur to the status of the Knight Grand Cross of the Most Distinguished Order of St. Michael and St. George in June 2010, from his 2001 status of Knight Commander of the Order of St. Michael and St. George.

Arthur Alexander Foulkes was born in Mathew Town, Inagua, May 11, 1928, the son of the late Dr. William A. Foulkes and Mrs. Julie Foulkes nee Maisonneuve.

He was educated at public schools in Matthew Town and Nassau and worked at The Nassau Guardian as a linotype operator and proof-reader. He joined The Tribune as a linotype operator in 1948 and took up journalism under Editor and Publisher Sir Etienne Dupuch who made him a reporter and later appointed him News Editor of The Tribune.

Sir Arthur was founding editor of Bahamian Times, official organ of the Progressive Liberal Party from 1962 to 1967.

Arthur Hanna.

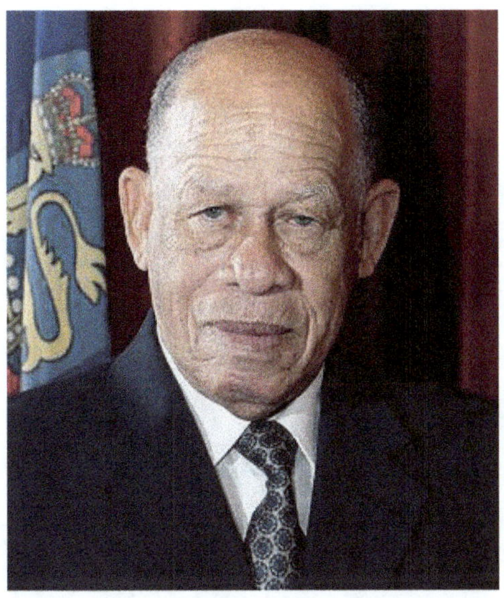

Hanna has been active in Bahamian politics since the 1950s. As a member of the Progressive Liberal Party, Hanna represented the Ann's Town, Nassau constituency as a MP in the Bahamas' House of Assembly from 1960 to 1992.

During this time, Hanna assumed a number of important cabinet posts, including Deputy Prime Minister of the Bahamas from 1967 to 1984.

In 1984, Hanna resigned his post as Deputy to Prime Minister Lynden Pindling in protest at the retention by Pindling of cabinet colleague who were heavily criticized by a Royal Commission of Enquiry of that same year. The Commission was established to investigate claims of high-level corruption allegedly linked to the flourishing drugs trade of the 1980s.

His resignation came within a week of the firing from the Cabinet of Hubert Ingraham and Perry Christie, who also were

said to have taken a strong stand against the presence in the
cabinet of ministers tarnished by the commission and who both
later served successive terms as Prime Minister

Hubert Ingraham

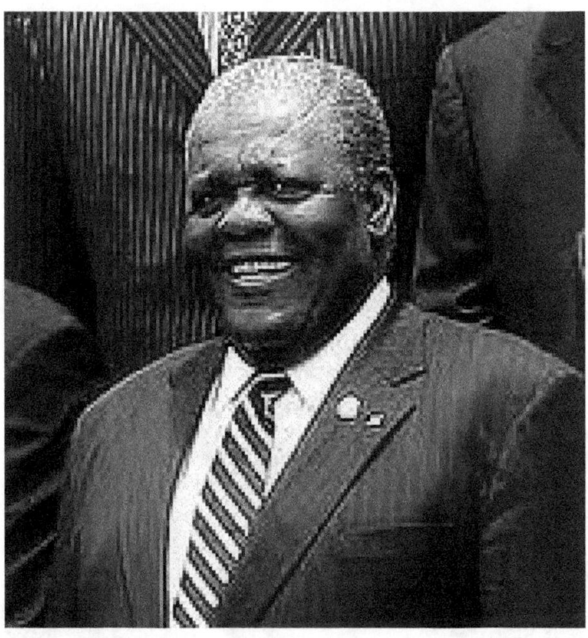

Remarks by Rt. Hon. Hubert A. Ingraham Party Leader FNM Inagua Rally Wednesday 2 May, 2012

Good Evening Inagua, Colour Red is very happy to be in Inagua tonight. We have spent the day in MICAL visiting with residents in Crooked Island, Acklins and Mayaguana. Last evening Colour Red was in Central Andros.

All are excited. They are fired up and ready to join the red wave that has covered all of the Family Islands. I told them I was coming to Inagua to visit with some old friends and to welcome some new ones who have determined to join us this time and help us make history by voting for Sydney Collie and making him the MP for MICAL on Monday 7th May.

Sidney Collie

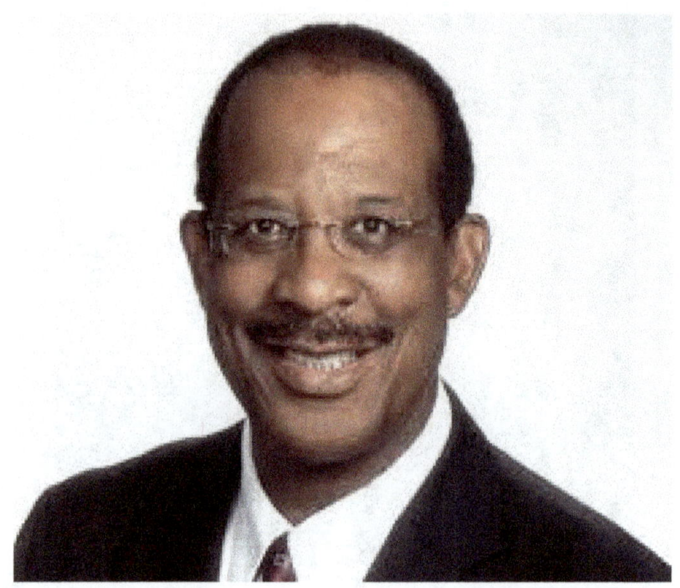

Inagua, MICAL bought the bag of promises being sold by that other Party on two successive occasions and got nothing for its effort. In fact, we almost lost Mayaguana as a result. Had the wheeler dealers in that other Party gotten their way, more than 10,000 acres of Mayaguana would be under foreign control today with minimum benefit coming to the Bahamian people. We put an end to that and returned some 6,000 of those acres back to the Bahamian Crown Land bank.

You will have had the opportunity to look at our Manifesto 2012 and to compare it with that other Party's election platform. True to form, you will have found reasoned, planned commitments set out in Manifesto 2012. We take our responsibility to you, the Bahamian people, seriously.

The same cannot be said for that other Party. They have made it their trademarks to overpromise and under-deliver. Their platform is a book filled with their Leader's dreams and empty promises. No one should rely on them. Experience has proven to all; even to many in their own Party, that a promise from Perry can only lead to "Delivery Failed"! They failed to deliver on most of their promises in their single term in office; now they are promising to set in motion a truck load of new initiatives in their first 100 days if returned to office. Don't be fooled – their book of dreams is nothing more than fool's gold; it will all tarnish.

Indeed, it would tarnish before the completion of those fabled first 100 days of promised action. And that is even when we take into account that their promises for the first 100 days don't actually set out any concrete action. Instead, it sets out what they will plan and or initiate or set in motion. I have only one question for that group: When do you propose to actually do something? But we all have the answer, don't we? Never! They are the Party of Never Ready and Late Again.

You know firsthand of which I speak, because your current MP has been most neglectful. Like most of that Gold Rush crew he is long on talk, but small on action. I use to marvel that he would get up in the House and say all kinds of things about what he had done or was going to do. The only problem is that it was all talk and little action. Remember all his big talk about hurricane relief some years ago? That other side talked about your new clinic forever. They botched up the job so we had to make it right. They either do-nothing or buss-up whatever they get their incompetent and greedy hands on.

If you want more talk, vote for him. But if you want action and to be a part of a Delivery Team, vote for Sydney Collie, vote FNM. This is my last election, Inagua. Come go with me. That other side will forget you. I will forget you not!

Inagua:

If you examine their Book of Promises you will discover nary an original or new idea. They have repackaged their old unfulfilled promises and decorated those with some ideas borrowed from us. You know how some people take the gift you give them for Christmas and repackage them because they forgot to go shopping. Well, this is exactly what most of the PLP platform looks like.

It must pain their supporters in these farthest reaches of our island chain that in their 2012 Book of Promises they say that they will look into the harvesting of cascarilla bark which is used in the creation of Campari. Well, they promised this back in 2002! Could they possibly believe that the people of MICAL have not noticed that they did absolutely nothing to even try and put such a programme in place during 5 long years in office between 2002 and 2007?

Believe you me; they are the same PLP, same empty promises. They are not serious. They are trifling with you and they're trifling with the future of our country. The sensible people of The Bahamas put them out after one disappointing term in office; Mayaguana and Crooked Island are coming with me this time; Acklins-maybe. I ask you to join in the tidal wave of Red covering our country; seal the deal for better, come with me Inagua and help us keep them out!

Remember Perry's Law: The more he promises, the less he'll deliver. I was happy just last month to visit you on the happy occasion of the opening of the new modern NIB Community Health Clinic. Regrettably, it was a poorly managed project set in train back in 2005 but which was so badly managed that it cost NIB some $3.5 million – almost 100% more than the Ministry of Works said it should cost back in 2005.

The development of community health clinics around the country is only one of the many important social development programmes of the National Insurance Board.

We are offering Sidney Collie as our candidate for election to the House of Assembly. He is a native son of MICAL; but unlike your present MP, he will look after your interest. He will be a representative of the ilk of your last FNM MP Mr. Vernon Symonette who served the nation with dignity and dedication as Speaker of the House of Assembly. Like Vernon, Sidney will make you proud.

Sidney Collie comes to you as a part of a delivery team. We take our jobs seriously. We are not in this for ourselves; we are here to make life better for all Bahamians. Take it from me – my record is long; it is public and I never seek to run from it. My record is one of deliverance.

Sidney is a part of an energetic team that has a good mixture of tried and tested experience candidates, professionals with specialists skills in the law, medicine, finance, agriculture, and business and youthful energy filled with innovative ideas. All are committed to continue our important work of making life better for you.

Sidney has served our Party and our Bahamian people in the House of Assembly and in the Senate. He is currently our non-resident Ambassador to Caricom where he has gained the respect of the region. He has my full confidence, and he has the full confidence of our Party. Now it is up to you to make him the next Member of Parliament from this constituency. Your current MP and his Party has taken you for granted for ten long years. He spent most of his time in the House looking after his own interests.

Did he use his time to come to see you, to attend to your needs, to your community's needs and to see after your development? Unfortunately, no, he did none of that! He has spent his time looking after himself and seeking out opportunities for himself. You need an MP who will work for you! And Sidney is that man. It's time that you had a Member of Parliament who puts your needs and your interests, your dreams and your aspiration in the forefront of his agenda.

Sidney is fired up about programs like Self Starter and Jump Start, put in place by the FNM Government since 2007, to provide essential seed funding to independent entrepreneurs and small business owners.

Inagua some 48 individuals on this island have been engaged in the 52 week National Jobs Readiness and Skills Training Programme. Participants have been placed in a cross section of private businesses and public corporations.

4,000 Bahamians in Nassau, in Grand Bahama, and the Family Islands are participating in the programme receiving training and work experience which could land them permanent jobs and which will definitely better prepare them to find and qualify for jobs in the economy. I want to encourage young people to take advantage of all the programmes the Government has developed to give talented Bahamians a "leg up" so to speak. Make the programmes work for you.

Inagua: Putting Bahamians First is a duty I have sworn to uphold each time I placed my hand on the Bible and promised to abide by the constitution and protect the interests of Commonwealth of The Bahamas.

That other Party is good at framing glib slogans to try and catch people's imaginations. They also have a long record of disappointing those who buy into their slogans. In this campaign they believe in Bahamians and promise to invest in Bahamians. Regrettably, they're only slogans.

When given the opportunity to believe in Bahamians and to invest in Bahamian between 2002 and 2007 they chose otherwise. They cancelled the government subsidy of ½ interest payable on government guaranteed educational loans introduced by the FNM; they failed to build a single new school or library. Inagua deserves more than empty PLP promises and slogans.

Fellow Bahamians: After a number of years during which you were speared the wrath of summer hurricanes you have been visited by terrible storms in recent time, most dramatically when Hurricane Ike made a direct strike on this island. Notwithstanding the considerable damage to property, I think we were very fortunate to have escaped with no serious injury. I know that the experience would have brought you a new appreciation for the men and women of the Royal Bahamas Police Force and the Royal Bahamas Defence Force who are invaluable parts of our emergency first responder team. And very personally, you will know the benefit of our having established a Defence Force base here in Inagua. As you know the new Base at Ragged Island is now virtually complete.

Located here, in the far southern reaches of our island chain, you also appreciate the important work of the Defence Force in protecting our marine borders, and acting to stop illegal contraband including narcotic drugs and guns, poaching and illegal immigration. As a part of our National Security Strategic Plan, we will dredge the harbor at the Inagua Defence Force base to allow for larger vessels. Inagua is a critical part of our forward-positioning of various Defense Force assets. We plan also to construct a facility here in Inagua to store hurricane relief supplies for the Southern Bahamas. You are also a critical part of our hurricane relief and recovery plans.

We also plan to develop a base in Grand Bahama, and sub-bases in Abaco and Exuma.

Those of you who have had the opportunity to review Manifesto 2012 which is now available on line as well as in printed form; will see that my Government has given and continues to give priority attention to beefing up our ability to confront these ills on all fronts.

The FNM's decision to transform the Royal Bahamas Defense Force was done with great deliberation and plenty hard thinking. It will be the largest, boldest, and most wide-scale boost of the Force in its entire year history.

We undertook extensive studies on the organization and strength of the Defense Force. We appointed a group of eight former and serving Defense Force Commanders and Captains to advise on what was required in terms of vessels and manpower.

The Experts Committee provided advice on the correct number of vessels and the manpower levels required for the Force to adequately fulfill its mandate to patrol our waters and to enforce our laws with respect to fisheries, legal entry and trade.

Today's Force strength is 1164. We want to take it to 1,400 men. We have calculated that over the next five years approximately 40 marines may leave the Force for a variety of reasons. This will require that we recruit more than 235 additional personnel in order to achieve and maintain Force strength of 1,400 marine.

The professional, reasoned advice we received helped us to form and make our determinations on recruitment and the acquisition of vessels. It also informed our decision to create a Defense Force Reserve.

With regard to protecting our seas and resources, those who oppose us simply adjusted some of our numbers upwards and proclaimed it their plan. This from the Never-Ready Government that over a five-year term in office bought a single aircraft, which was completely unsuitable for patrol exercises, and not a single vessel to outfit the Royal Bahamas Defense Force. Now he says he will do more than we project. This from a Never-Ready government which took almost 4 years to appoint a Commodore of the Defense Force.

Inagua: The FNM is a big tent party; we take in all who want better for The Bahamas. I say to all good thinking and loyal Inaguans, come with me, and support my Party the FNM; we have and keep your interest at heart. That is why not a single public servant was disengaged as a result of the global economic downturn. That is why, notwithstanding the impact of the global economic recession upon our economy, we, the FNM government, increased social service assistance, expanded NIB benefit programmes and engaged additional Policemen, Defense Force marines, immigration and customs officers. Those others are busy trying to deflect attention from their weak leader; trying desperately to convince the Bahamian population that this election is not about leadership. You know better.

Elections in difficult economic times demand that leadership be a principal issue. These are times for strong and decisive leadership; leadership that will make the tough choices. This is no time for wavering and waffling. This is no time for talk and more talk. This is a time for action.

I offer you on behalf of the proven leadership of the Free National Movement. I offer you accountable and transparent government. I offer you clean hands. I pledge again to you a Government that will deliver. We believe that Inagua will benefit from The Heritage Tourism Initiative which will create jobs and boost your economy.

As the site of an important Inagua National Park and home to the largest flock of Flamingoes, Inagua stands to benefit from this initiative which will facilitate the upgrade of the infrastructure needed to enhance heritage sites and the heritage experience that residents and tourists are able to enjoy during such visits. This initiative will encourage both Bahamian and international tourist to visit and help make their travel here easier. It is ripe with opportunities for residents to partner with the Bahamas National Trust in developing accommodations for visitors to the Park. The most revered National Trust guides and park wardens hail from Inagua so the blueprint already exists. Clearly there are opportunities for employment as tour guides that will be of interest to young people here in Inagua.

Inagua:

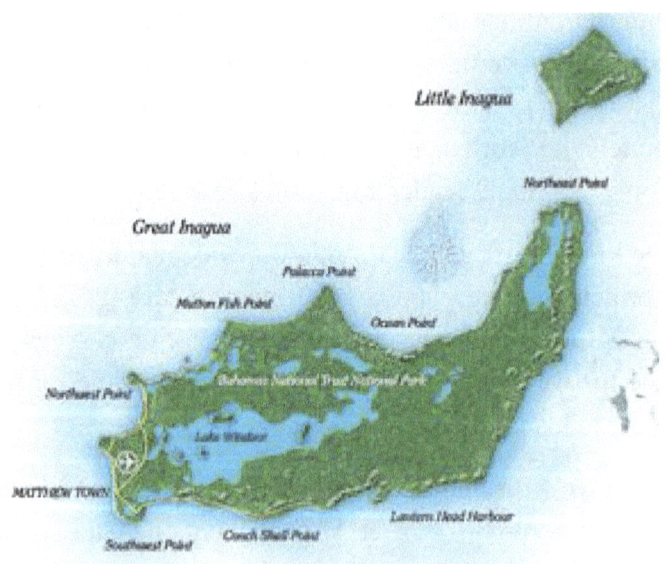

It is the FNM that started the concept of promoting the various Islands of The Bahamas as unique destinations. We will continue to do so and this will include Inagua. We also have plans that will make it easier for passengers around the world to more easily book flights straight through to the Family Islands. We also want to make it easier for school children from the Capital to travel to Inagua and other Family Islands to see for themselves important historic and cultural sites. Inagua is the last outpost of commercially produced salt in The Bahamas. The salt industry runs through most of our existence yet only the smallest number of Bahamian school children have had the opportunity to see the white mountains of salt, to see the salt pans rich with the pink shrimp, a major food source for the flamingoes contributing to their rich pink Colour. We also have plans to see how The Bahamas can take greater advantage of mariculture and aquaculture, both of which have to do with the cultivation of various marine life for food and other purposes.

Moreover, how might some of the salt pans be utilized in ecotourism such as salt baths, which the world over have been known for medicinal and healing purposes. I know that some people have been talking for a number of years, how some of the salt plans can be added for tourism and health purposes that will add value to the vital salt industry here. Seeing and understanding these things help build national pride and respect for all things Bahamian.

It is the FNM that will make sure that much of the best kept secret of Inagua is shared with more Bahamians and visitors who will come to see the richness of your natural and historical heritage. You are among a select number of Family Islands to have been the birthplace of a Governor General. We need to showcase more of your rich history.

Inagua: FNMs: It is the FNM that will always look after the interest of the Family Islands. That is why we introduced Local Government; expanded the electricity and telephone infrastructure, made access to cable TV possible, constructed modern community health clinics close to Family Island population centres, undertook large scale infrastructural upgrades around the country: roads, bridges, docks, ports, schools all receiving focused attention, many after long years of neglect by other administrations. We are reconstructing and paving your roads, some for the first time ever at a cost of $3.6 million. This is the second time that I have undertaken the upgrade of your roads. We met them in terrible condition in 1992 and we fixed them. The job was not as well done as we had expected. This time we have contracted Mr. Symonette out of Eleuthera and we are satisfied that he will do a good job for you so that we do not have to revisit this for many years to come.

We also provided Local Government with some $200,000 to facilitate a number of small projects important to the life of your residents. These projects include the clearing and renovation of your drainage system, the repair and reconstruction of seawalls, the replacement of three public cabanas, improvements to the Over-the-Hill Park, the reconstruction of Market Place including the renovation of public restrooms, repairs to the Lighthouse, the construction of Heroes' Park and the cleaning and maintenance of the historic cemetery which is no longer in use.

Since 2007 we caused BEC to assume responsibility for the energy grid on this island resulting in a 30% increase in electricity production on this island. And that is why we have refocused attention on regularizing the occupation and accelerating consideration of new applications by Bahamians for Crown land. Since 2007 alone, some 27 applications have been approved for residents of Inagua.

Those others made plans to sell off acres and acres of Bahamian land to foreign interest to build, tax free, luxury homes for international persons. We believe that the first call on Crown

Land must be for the benefit of Bahamians. We have no objection to the long lease and sale of Crown Lands to foreign parties if it is for the development of productive economic activity that will employ Bahamians and bring true development to our people. Development of a hotel, a manufacturing plant, an assembly facility, these are developments to be encouraged and promoted and assisted but not building luxury homes tax The FNM always places the highest priority on education – on expanding facilities, improving tuition materials, increasing the numbers of teachers and providing an unprecedented number of scholarships.

I want to confirm that we have completed the planning for the construction of a new school for Inagua replacing the one so badly damaged by the Hurricane Ike that it had to be abandoned. The school will have 6 standard classrooms and four specialists' labs – one each for home economics, woodwork, sewing and science, a library and a computer classroom and then the regular administrative block and restroom facilities for students. The renovation of a single story building at the back of the school will permit it to be converted into art and music classrooms. And the school will have covered walkways. The school construction project has been budgeted at a cost of some $6.8 million. I give you my undertaking that the school will be built early in our next term in office. When the FNM promise you can believe it because the FNM DELIVERS!

We have also ensured that our teachers are properly equipped with tuition materials so that no child is disadvantaged in the classroom.

The Government has also agreed to pay 80 per cent of the health insurance premium for teachers in the Government operated school system; teachers will pay 20 per cent. This new benefit enters into effect with the new Budget on 1st. July of this year. In our next term we will build additional COB dormitory space in New Providence to accommodate family island students and we will provide rental stipends to needs tested students who cannot be accommodated in the dormitories. Those others lie when they tell you that they believe in young Bahamians. They believe only in helping themselves, their families and their friends.

Inagua: In transforming our country we cannot go with the smallness of vision and the weakness of leadership of the PLP. Not only will they take the country backwards; they lack the vision and the quality of leadership needed to move The Bahamas forward. But, this is not a fight any of us can go alone, we must band together. So tonight, sign up to be a volunteer, take a poster, tell your friends to go FNM and when you go to our website tonight, we'd be grateful if you would click the donate button and help us keep printing posters and making t-shirts and holding rallies.

Time is near. I ask all voters to pick up their cards as soon as possible and have information corrected on it if this is necessary. As we depart tonight FNMs, I ask you, come go with me and the FNM. Vote for Sidney; make him your next MP. He will look after your interest and he will make you proud. Inagua together, let us build a better Bahamas.

Thank you, God bless The Bahamas, and good night

Wounded Children Faces of Triumph

The Bahamas and its standing in Caribbean affairs; the financial position, cultural and legal systems and its developing struggles are incomplete since independence.

The government and peoples' character and current political leadership are all interwoven with the nature of world politics.

The Bahamian model or rather the Pindling model, featured economic inter-activities and various political schemes and contradictions geared to attract wealthy outsiders to advance economic development and commerce for the people of the Family islands.

Though the model did earlier eliminate many disparities and inequalities, forced upon the people by the old regime(s); (i.e.) 1950 – 1967.

The Bahamas was discovered on 12 October 1492, during Columbus' first voyage, but was settled by Spaniards during the first decades of the sixteenth century. The islands had no real usefulness to Spain, other than used as a staging ground for other expedition throughout the West Indies, but the role was greatly enhanced during the American civil war and later with the rum running period through north America and the Caribbean.

With the English occupation of Havana 1762 -1763, new opportunities for trade emerged and with Nassau's' linkage to Britain, North America and the Caribbean contributed to the influx of new political ideas, customs and other forms of organizations.

The prevailing mercantilist philosophy was grounded in the belief that the accumulation of wealth was a necessary ingredient of natural power, giving rise to influential groups of people, promoting capitalist ideas and productions, while slavery and colonialism did not impede efforts to improve the emerging Bahamian cultural life.

Educational opportunities were restricted by birth, wealth and privilege. Though double standards prevailed regarding social status of males in the society in which Blacks and women were decidedly subordinate.

Many years of bitter political conflict ensued but the goal of political independence was achieved following "self-government" from Great Britain in the mid nineteen sixties.

American interests in the Bahamas, namely Nassau and Freeport (Grand Bahamas), expanded dramatically in the early years of the Pindling period.

Investments and commerce predates the transformation in American society wrought by the rise of industrial centers and monopolistic fortunes of the new American financial explorers.

Political involvement in the internal Bahamas politics was largely restricted to commercial matters up until 1983, when American (DEA) Drug Enforcement Agency got acutely involved in investigating the apparent trans-shipment of illicit drugs through the islands to many other places, namely the U.S; however U.S enforcement of neutrality was generally casual up to this point in the islands' history.

Though with times it peaked with overzealous Ambassadors attempting to influence partisan matters, but having been rejected they normally conformed to the traditional roles assigned to Emissaries.

Meanwhile going into a script of political order under the leadership of Sir Lynden O. Pindling, first Prime Minister of the Bahamas, who singlehandedly brought global respect for the Bahamian people and country.

While I believed the people had only partially understood the constitutionality of the white paper etched during the London conference on independence. An attempt is made to show what was compelled upon the people instead.

The historical objectives of a free, independent and fully sovereign democratic nation was largely unrealized under the Progressive Liberal Party , (PLP) and the 300,000 people was still subjected to the authority of foreign powers through the pretense of tourism as an natural national industry.

Despite epic improvement in health, education, sanitation, public administration, economic and finance achieved under the Pindling tutelage, the failure to expand (I.A.C) Islandistical Autonomous Councils and inter-government to the Family islands created lingering tensions of repression and resentment in Nassau from Family islanders complicating inter-island relationships and stability from fomenting.

The more Nassau comes to depend on tourism, the less possibility there is going to be wider economic diversity throughout the islands.

The Bahamas dependence will increase and we shall be completely and hopelessly at the mercy of large hotel/motel owners and associations, whose interests remains largely focus in Nassau/Freeport and with multi-national corporations coffer not particularly advancing to the natives.

The day the Bahamas becomes one big tourist destination, the national sovereignty will vanish.

PLP reforms following Pindlings' victory 1967 with Sir Randal Fawkes, led to rising expectations and surging Bahama-nationalism

Sir Pindling approach centered initially on impressive public works programs and attempts at economic diversification in the island of New Providence namely.

Hopes were dashed, when apparently constitutional norms were allegedly violated and stifled as electoral victories were secured from the opposition during the late 1970s and 1980s, through electoral gerrymandering.

However, election courts never ever proved that any fraud did actually occur.

That's a fact some people say.

The forces arrayed against Sir Pindling vibrant like web were heterogeneous in nature, with daring tactics and often ideologically opposed to each other earlier on. Amongst the genesis were the Free PLPs led by Sir Wallace Withfield a politically ambitious genius.

Even though the romantic immaturity of the PLP generation brought about much depletion of national motivation as cynicism of community fostered openly and patronage w an acceptable form of pay back.

No doctrine of constructive friendship or dialogue was ever employed and encouraged by the PLP hierarchy with nationals outside of their ranks.

Nuestra Razon (Our Purpose) was political independence and wider economic prosperity and hope was never fully realized under the PLP 1969 – 1982.

Revolutionary changes of restructuring class, property, political, civil rights, gender equality, economic, foreign and inter-island-policy and commerce and regional affairs confronts any new Prime Minister, who must work to eliminate the dependence on tourism and broaden the nature the tourist-dollars could contribute to the opening of many other economic inter-activities and political autonomous models for the islanders.

Not that such is inherently corrupt it must take into account the very nature of the archipelago while broadening the scope of financial linkages throughout the Commonwealth for all the inhabitants to embrace.

The Inside Story...
"It's Better In the Bahamas"

The unspeakable calamity this poor province suffers from pirates obliges me to inform your lordship of it. Gov. Robert Johnson 1717.

The Frezel had only minutes earlier dropped anchor off the west point of the island, not far away from the deep water seaport town called Betsy Bay; perhaps for the last time, following a couple of days sheltering at Porter's Cay dock in Nassau, due mostly to the dismal weather conditions in the Exuma Cays.

Residents were mostly pleased that their beloved native Captain and crewmen were all safe along with the cargo.

The captain knew most residents were going to be glad he had no trouble with the Cuban/Russian frigates that plied very close to the islands, normally without incidents, but this time was different.

The Americans had landed and occupied the airbase near Abraham's Bay, the capital of the sparsely populated Mayaguana. Besides, rumors were everywhere, Mr. Bernard Depuch, Member of Parliament (UBP); was on his way through Pirates Well to see United Bahamian Party supporters, but many residents thought out loudly, it was an affront; Mr. Bernard Depuch was ferried about with numerous U.S troops not too far behind his entourage.

Even old folks asked openly, what's next, remembering President Fulgencio Battista's' (1952 – 1959) carnage in Cuba ending and the "New Jack Warrior " named Fidel Castro riding high in Havana, maybe it was not so bad after all having the Americans in town. But what next? Would the Americans keep the Cuban/Russians advances at bay?

No one knew for sure, but the news was caliente caliente everywhere, Mr. Bernard Depuch could not say for sure either, why sixty nine hundred American GI's were patrolling the beaches and waterway, around islands of MICAL. What was next?

Early in the morning gun shots were heard. The troops drove through the beachfront town of Pirates Well, stopping at the lone convenient store, dropping off many dead U.S presidents for food stuffs, but few residents interfaced with the occupying troops. Even though there were days the daughters of many residents were hidden from the GI's view.

Then the Mr. Bernard Depuch sent word out that there was no need to "be alarm", even with numerous aerial frequencies of jets landing and taking off; some community operatives with the local Constable were suspicious crazy, as they listened to ZNS Radio, though villagers could barely hear what Radio Bahamas were saying, through the distortions and static sounds, news surfaced of missiles in Cuba pointing at the U.S mainland only procreated more fear.

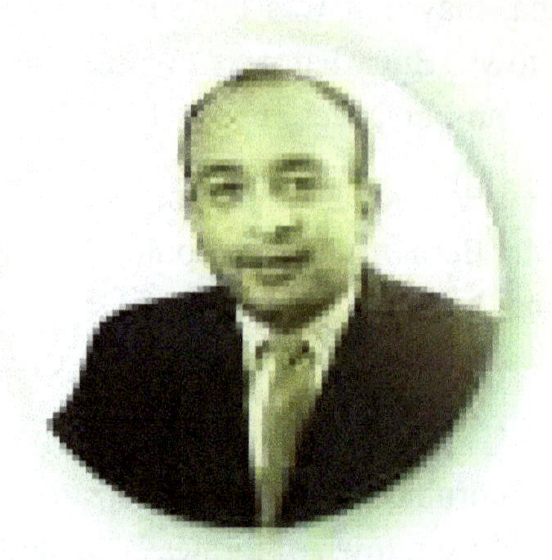

BERNARD C. H. DUPUCH
Born: 21st January, 1903
Died: 12th June, 2004
Age: 81 years

Real or perceived, some islanders clustered around the short-wave radio and heard President John F. Kennedy chided the Cubans to get the Russian missiles the hell out.

What next? With the artificial linkage to Nassau, news were tangled up more, that President Khrushchev had sent submarines that had missiles on board that would blow up the islands in four nano seconds; much more these submarines were armed and dangerous with nuclear warheads, aimed at Miami, Washington, D.C, New York and San Francisco.

What was next was the prevailing consensus around Cuba's insistence and Russian intransigence, islanders began to ask where were the Americans storing their weapons that may have had plutonium, radio-active agents and other low level biological contaminants?

Was it at the airbase near Abraham's Bay? The Captain knew quite well residents were scared and sought out the Mr. Bernard Depuch; but was most unsuccessful only to find out later that Mr.

Bernard Depuch too, had no clue, but he did promise to get answers from Sir Stafford Sand (UBP) and Sir Roland Symonette (UBP). Already sixty two days had elapsed, the U.S troops were everywhere with public beach landings in Pirates Well and Betsy Bay.

The Mr. Bernard Depuch (MP) could not say anything affirmative, but the Captain of the Frezel knew Mr. Cleophas Adderley (UBP) and sought out his help only to be told some classified tests were being conducted on the island.

The people were generally friendly but worried about these military tests being conducted throughout the island and in the ocean around the MICAL.

Again the Member of Parliament showed up on a British Airways flight from Nassau, some five months later with an answer, that the Americans were "positioned in Mayaguana to assist in neutralizing the U.S.S.R advances."

Not many residents doubted him, though some had began to talk about how the United Bahamian Party (UBP) had dispatched a number of medical aides to check "all" school aged children for unspecified and un-named ailments.

The medical aides administered to the children a cube of white sugar with a few drops of a red colored substance and ordered mouth to be "opened wide" and digest the sugar cube. Some were also given vaccinations.

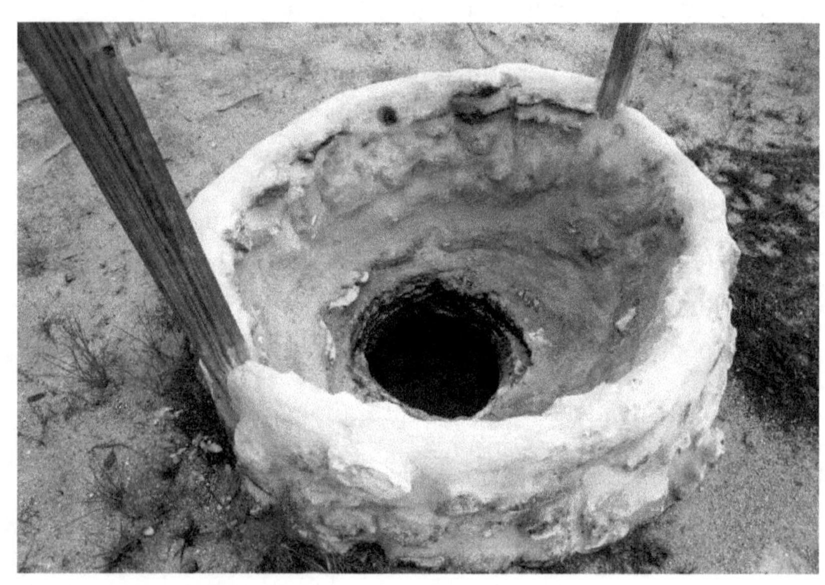

Pirates Well Mayaguana Bahamas

Fault Lines

Should the constitution of the Bahamas remain a United Kingdom order, or should it be a document enacted by the Bahamas House of parliament?

Should the Bahamian constitution specially outline "Civil Rights?"

Should the child of a Bahamian married female have the same constitutional rights as the child of a single/married Bahamian male?

Is it right for the residents of New Providence (Nassau) to be denied the right to have a local government body like their counterparts in the Family islands?

Should the Bahamian Supreme Court, Magistrate Judges and other Judiciary be comprised solely of indigenous Bahamians?

What level of Jurisprudence is practiced in the Bahamas, if any?

Can the Bahamian Supreme court be viewed as a bulwark of Justice?

Is it necessary to attach additional constitutional safeguards or amendments so as to guarantee autonomy for the Family islands?

Does the Supreme Court of the Bahamas have the right or power to review legislations for constitutional conformity?

Should all arrested persons be read their constitutional rights?

Should a child a birth, be given a National Insurance number and right to citizenship?

Should the protection against discrimination be extended to include categories such as: Disability, catastrophic diseases, examples H.I.V, A.I.D.S, Alzheimer's/Parkinson's and others not presently defined in the vernacular?

Should the death penalty, which is codified in the article of the constitution, be abolished?

Should the minimum wage be raised to reflect the prevailing consensus that allows one to live reasonably well in the present environment known to all Bahamians?

Should the Central government provide without malice, legal representation as a civil right for all detainees?

Should the government place more emphasis on "National security" to include issues relating to immigration, border patrol/control, mass transportation and emigration?

Does the Prime Minister have the power to dissolve the House at any time?

Does the Constitution provide a method for smooth removal of Members of Parliament for specific reasons that may be deemed inappropriate to national norms?

Should impeachment proceedings be a plank in the constitution?

Should there be an official residence and official place of business for the "sitting" Prime Minister during tenure?

Should a port authority board be assigned or appointed to oversee the metropolitan transit issue in New Providence and throughout the country?

Should the public transportation system be immediately classified as a national security matter effectively nationalizing the same?

Should the election be held on a certain month and certain day every five years?

Example: Every five years on the second Wednesday of May or Second Saturday and Sunday of July?

Setting Up a National Security Council

(NSCB)

It is without any doubt I supported the Sovereign on the issue of immigration. My sentiments are known well by many. Firstly the sovereign must secure the islands from Great Inagua to the Berry islands.

How do we deal with this one might ask?

The National Security Council will function to advise and assist the Prime Minister and the Interior Minister on matters of national security and foreign policies. The Council will be set up to assist in coordinating these precise policies among various arms of the government. The NSC is chaired by the Prime Minister only or as the Prime Minister assigned an Interlocutor/Operative.

Each island should have two – four members who sit on the National Security Council for a term not longer than four to six years with monthly payment for service.

1. The hiring of special security agents who will roam the respective territories, filing daily reports on what was seen, heard as they move about the islands, sea and beaches and the interior.

2. All nationals crafts that ply the waters of the Bahamas must have an implanted device that Control and Command could interface with at all times.

3.   This implanted devise will be planted for a fee which will last for approximately two years. At the end of the two year period established by an act of Parliament and codified into law.

4.   All nationals are responsible for the islands' security. If you see something says something. Report to the known national security representative assigned to that island which is then forwarded to the appropriate Control and Command Unit.

5.   The national government must have targeted island forums to hear and to inform islanders of the concerns that must be made known to all.

6.   Establish certain zones that immigrants may be processed

These are some of the pivotal areas of concerns that needs to be addressed soon.

7.   Regular weekly reports are to be forwarded to the (N.S.C). National Security Council.

8.   Drone Technology that is for air, land and sea usages and cultivated and explored by the N.S.C and assigned agents to perform various national duties as deemed by Command.

9.   Set up Assistant Attorney General for the region to have power to check enforcement of rights and constitutional compliance

Faces of Triumph

The many faces of the suffering people among the privileged political personalities that roam the landscape called the Commonwealth of the Bahamas, are not easily noticed by those who are in the non-targeted population.

It is heart wrenching to be awakened to the pain of the struggling people who have to scrap up, fish or cut bait for their daily survival and find that many who are the privileged do not show care or empathy for those who are helpless, hungry and may have "given-up" on getting ahead in this country.

This is visible with the VAT (Value Added Tax) discourse(s) and displayed intoxicatingly well by the privileged and political elites who even with a "Civil Service" weekly or monthly paycheck can never identify with or even understand why some people worry about how to feed their empty stomach calling out for food daily.

In the islands of the Bahamas there is little talk about the bias, disrespectful or even the perjurious politicians, preachers, boss men and women who go about their business knowing full well that the unfair way so many people are treated is not "Godly" and never could or even say a word of rebuke.

No matter the xenophobic higher-ups, coworkers who display occasional behavior not defined as conducive for cohesive national honor of fair-play, decency and partnership that as natives to this land are all endowed with rights that are not always equal as we would like "rights" to be; but still many exhibit the "better than thou" disposition that is pervasive throughout the country.

Of course many people have been working on these traits and leanings and seek to eradicate the nurtured disparaging and xenophobic attitude.

Key:

A value-added tax (VAT) is a tax on the sales of goods and services to consumers. However, unlike a traditional retail sales tax that is collected only on final sales to consumers, a VAT is collected from businesses at each stage of the production process.

Biases are human tendencies that lead us to follow a particular quasi-logical path, or form a certain perspective based on predetermined mental notions and beliefs. When investors act on a bias, they do not explore the full issue and can be ignorant to evidence that contradicts their initial opinions.

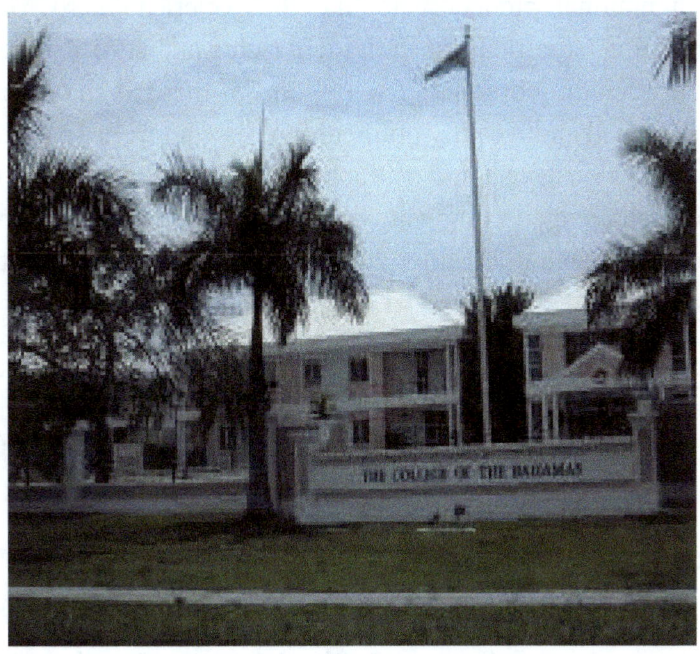

The College of The Bahamas

The Forgotten Islander

When principal Mr. Hugh Campbell, walked the halls of Balliou High school back in the days, Blue hill road in New Providence, Bahamas in the summer of 1971; students revered his eloquence, his awesomely stern candor and his ability to instill calmness, honor and dignity of service as a duty to country, to each other and to function with a sense of what students had to do as young people for the new and emerging independent nation.

Most students loved and praised his fatherly tenure at the school.

By the time I had become a senior. I too admired for the first time a national pioneer who like the American hero Martin Luther King, stood tall for individual rights and equality against the masquerading practices and policies of the British led group of entrenched and wealthy political figures who from 1640 to the late 1960's enslaved and entrapped the local population in a racially challenged composite and denied the people fair play, justice and economic rights for the Afric-Bahamians and their descendants.

With the advent of self-government Bahamians now could all gather around a passionate and pronounced leader, named Lynden O. Pindling, who spoke with such fluency and candidly about a new concept of island nationalism?

Young student relished in the fact that "This land is our land., from Great Inagua to the Berry islands." We all proudly sung.

Whatever was to become, Balliou High school students knew full well that this man spoke for our generation and for the first time in our lifetime students were going to have a voice in this country.

We will all proudly rise and say "All the way" because our time had come as this God sent gentleman who later became the beloved Prime Minister by an act again of God in 1968, spoke with such conviction and fervor, began the monumental task of re-structuring a new and vibrant country for all of the people; wrestled with Harold Wilson the British Prime Minister and demanded Independence from the Crown which was celebrated July 10th 1973

I remember well when 'my' Prime Minister now Sir Lynden O. Pindling used words like " proclivity", "economic parity" and "social justice", I knew then that we were finally liberated from the chains of oppression and so the promise of growth, fair play, justice and progressive development would be shared by all from Great Inagua to the Berry islands.

Now some forty odd years have passed as I wait relief from the political victimization and the heinous and acute denial of justice, compensation, likely civil service seniority and an apology from the national regime, because I at the time called for an (ASP) Alternate Solution Plan to halt and combat undue hardship heaped upon opponents and believed for open political discourse to foster and birth growth inferred that the (BSC) Bahamas Supreme Court could be utilized, through a supposed judicial remedy or safeguard called "an injunction" to help guarantee elements of reasonable-ness for political dialogue(s) for locals.

In 1975, two years of independence, dressed with national pride and an open mind and working as a teacher, following a brief orientation at the then Teacher's college in Oakes field, Nassau Bahamas, joined with the Hon Edmund Moxey in a call for the economic pie to be shared more equitably with the people from Over the Hill ,

Following demonstration in front of the House of Assembly and then later denied employment when returning back to Yellow Elder primary school fall of 1975 as principal Mrs. Thelma Ford echoed that the public statements made in support of the above mentioned Member of Parliament was not in the national interest and that I had to go to the Ministry of Education headquarters for further instructions.

At the time I recognized with blunt clarity that the sovereign Bahamas constitution proclaims and guaranteed fundamental human rights, freedom of conscience, expression and assembly; while protecting privacy and expressly prohibited deprivation of the same, but did not make any reference(s) to the " civil rights" of any national of the country.

Meanwhile many of the political operatives and appointees of the Ministry of Education with the Hon. Livingstone Coakley as the Cabinet Minister had begun to execute patterns and practices to purge any and all questionings of anyone who shown support for the Hon Edmund Moxeys' view for the Coconut Grove revitalization plan and development 1972 – 1975.

As Back Bench Member of Parliament it was customary that either submission or total loyalty had to be visibly shown towards the government and no dissent was looked upon favorably.

As Parliament sat the duly elected Member for Mayaguana and Inagua the Hon Joseph Ford (P.L.P) continued a campaign of disenfranchisement and victimization of people and families of people who did not vote for him were all deemed unfavorably and could not gain viable employment or educational scholarship for colleges at home or foreign. That wasn't all. But moving pass that bump in the road became challenging no doubt.

Even though my views were always progressive and liberally inclusive I frequently wrote letters to the Editors of local newspapers and decried the pace of economic dislocation of people from the islands of Mayaguana, Inagua, Acklins and Crooked islands from 1969 – 1974.

With the passing of time, I yearned to give this lingering and nagging matter closure; and that the many historical misdeeds of the early years following the July 10th 1973 political release from the British may be truthfully and comprehensively viewed.

I retain the belief in the innate premise of human equality, civil rights and fair play under the rule of law may be acknowledged.

The silence of injustice cries out from the hill top seeking justice as I stood behind the grey curtains I said a prayer.

We shall overcome too.

Uriah McPhee

Uriah McPhee was a champion of the Bahamian struggle for independence long before it was popular. Courageous in the cause of liberty and passionate against the cruelty of the United Bahamian party a.k.a Bay Street Gang (BSG); functioning as the British styled cronies primarily in New Providence island as a stronghold.

Since his departure, numerous enactments have surfaced to marginalize the flow of information supplied to the masses fomented by PLP practices.

As the islanders developed a myopia view of government, they're very likely to see all other issues in a defoliated state of mind.

The weakening of social justice parallels an underlying deterioration of local institutions and activities that once democratized the masses. This has created and fostered schism and lack of respect for the family.

Communities were once small enough to permit contact among different types of the citizenry.

In the past, inevitable errors were made as in growing pains – but in a forgiving way. During the early years 1959 – 1969, PLP hierarchy handled problems that were not particularly familiar in scope e.g., Bilateral and, signatory on and of conventions and then, how to forge "islandistical" i.e. native development and inter-island progress.

There were false starts, grievous mistakes and contradictory implements to protect 'minorities' and those sinking in the economic sand, the disabled and others needing basic human rights as per Helsinki Accord, August 1st, 1975.

What many implements did was to slow and retard nationwide growth and outrightly slowed inherent growth opportunities throughout the Commonwealth, as a result this direct linkage ushered in crime wave after crime wave, hegemonic scams and schemes grew.

Bahamians no longer live within sight of each other, visually or spiritually or attend the same churches, schools or watering holes, as the automobile has become a social as well as a mechanical capsule in which the rich and not so well off, Cable beach elites and the Over the Hillers go about in their separate ways, places of worship, while passing each other in unseeing insulation.

In New providence, public libraries are few and not well stocked, while bulletins are posted for tourists to visit hotels, events, clubs but not 'native' pride and history news items are few if any.

There is little interfacing or encouragement for natives to visit public properties as PLP government encouraged very little mix-up with tourists unless they worked within the tourism sector.

No doubt it is very likely in an urbanized community the jibes of personal contact will be weakened. True, that will happen as the islands become larger metropolitan communities, however, I believe with the surge for building Bahama-nationalism new libraries and national complexes- i.e. public facilities ought to be prioritized so the people of the now and beyond would be the children of the 1950s, that went through an unorganized pogrom, conscientiously or not that was skillfully designed to eliminate the development of intellectual growth.

Once upon a time, schools and community events were more than one going to church on Sunday. They'd been encouraged and nurtured institutions.

Since July 10th, 1973 many public sites had been allowed to deteriorate and then they'd been choked off their native 'psyche' staggering to withstand the pressures associated with the ruins.

In the meantime, some groups benefitted largely from the chaos.

The dominant had less in common with reaching the disposed and addressing the weaknesses in the chore of the social disorder.

Radio Bahamas as a medium has become a glue that held together individual aspiration of those that was able to afford the luxuries of the noblesse oblige.

History is not reassuring on the incidence of voluntary unselfishness among the welders of power, who are not held accountable for their actions.

We've seen and learned the absolute power of medicine men, bishops, Ayatollahs and the long ruling family clans have produced less justice in any country on earth so far, than shared power and accountability.

It was the morbid history of uninhibited power that led to the formation of the PLP in the first place to bring down the dominance of the United Bahamian Party (UBP) culture and to chase the British out of the islands.

The same is true to jostle the native spirit and procreate the national Bahamian colors so the people could again sing "Lift up your head, oh Bahama land."

Commercial control of radio waves/tv is not inherently bad. But less evil than any other system known so far. With narrow control whether by government or corporation, it is then subjected to prevailing imbalances. In the end, no group, certainly not political with much uniformity as a government, is sufficiently open and secure to reject the completeness of society's values and wishes.

Opportunity for political changes to smooth transition must be safeguarded at all cost. While freedom of speech must show the government that it must be responsive to the electorate and it is not political rejection for a government to be defeated.

Rejection of a political party does not mean rejection of a party per se.

Other ideas need to be implemented for the advancement of the nation as an archipelago, where legal precedents are established to help guide "our" reasonableness table and indexes.

Urgent Aims

Throughout the twentieth century, the policy of the United States in the Caribbean sea region, including the Bahamas Islands in the Atlantic ocean has been distinguished from the policy of Latin America by the apparent readiness and willingness to intervene militarily, overtly or covertly in support of what is deemed "national security interests" by Washington D.C.

However I always wondered why was diseases not a perceived concern to the national security operatives of the US government, this was my opinion after watching 1the polio scare in the islands of the Bahamas 1962 - 1945, Pirates Well Mayaguana long before we witnessed islanders being crippled by a diseases where in my mind was a disaster so Ucal and I with Rodney Collie talked about it as a national security concern that should be high on the agenda for the globe.

In the period from Roosevelt Corollary 1904, which pronounced the unilateral assumption of global police power, in the western hemisphere, up to the protection of the good neighbor policy 1934, US troops occupied openly in Cuba, Honduras, Panama, Haiti, Nicaragua, Santa Domingo and Mayaguana (Bahamas) 1957 – 1963, during the Fidel Castro scare, as well as confirming the acquisition of Puerto Rico as a colony.

During the first World War 1917, the U.S negotiated a 99-year lease from the British for bases in Jamaica, St. Lucia, Trinidad, Guyana and the Bahamas, mainly on the island of Andros, San Salvador and Mayaguana to name a few, thereby confirming what was already known and understood, the inability of the British to defend occupied territories.

In 1954 with the adoption of tenth Inter American conference, in Caracas, Venezuela of a resolution affirming the incompatibility of Marxism or Communism with the perceived inter American system of government, while an active period of intervention was renewed, directly against Guatemala, Cuba 1958 – 1963 and the Dominican Republic 1965.

Where designated, appropriate policies of destabilization, which is similar to intervention but distinguished from it by the primary reliance of "locals" as opposed to external forces to bring about desired results, were employed.

In the case of British Guyana 1962 -1964, Jamaica 1975 - 1978, Nicaragua 1968 – 1982, the Bahamas 1973 – 1985, alongside other paramilitary strategies at other times since 1979. Thus, direct and active concerns with the greater Caribbean area is a demonstrated fact of US foreign policy."

This is expressed not in the "ifs" of intervention but, as one former senior foreign operative on Caribbean matters, in the State Department openly stated it is the "where, when and how policy".

The legitimacy of such an interpretation of the Greater Caribbean area derives from the perception of the region as "Vital" to safeguard US interests and isolate communistic tendencies following World War Two.

In recent years, two major aspects have been emphasized by US officials, as giving ground for concern.

The first is initially related to the global military balance with the former Soviet Union and focused on the development of U.S submarine warfare capability to limit the deployment of Soviet naval forces in the greater Caribbean.

In the 1970's Henry Kissinger, diplomatically blocked the construction of a putative nuclear submarine base in Cuba, directly or indirectly by the surveillance system (SOSUS which in turn involves the maintenance of numerous bases in the region, mainly the Bahamas on Andros island (AUTEC)

The second focus on the marine route for strategic materials either trans-shipment through the Panama Canal or through the Atlantic oceans.

Of these oils is the most paramount. Venezuela and Mexico have considerable gas and oil resources, while all over the Caribbean there are significant offshore oil fields.

As important is the area's status as an oil refinery zone, for crude from Africa and the Middle East.

While 40 – 50% of the US oil requirements are met from external sources of which some 22% is refined outside of the US mainland and a greater part in the Caribbean Around 1969 of 1,858,000 barrels per day of refined oil entering the US; no less than 1,032,900 has been refined in the Caribbean and BOROC in the Bahamas.

Economic interests turn on US direct investment and the migration tourist nexus. Since 1945 as in the first instance the trend has been widespread involvement and encouragement of transnational corporations to become actively involved in every sector of Bahamian/Caribbean economy and markets.

Traditional interests in export agriculture (Sugar and banana, grapes and oranges) mining petroleum and bauxite) have been supplemented by banking, insurance, transportation, bridge building, hotel construction, manufacturing and road building, thereby reinforcing simultaneously both the dependence of these countries on the US balance of payment surplus while the migration tourist nexus refers to a very considerable flow of people.

There are thousands of US citizens who live and work or vacation in the islands, together constitutes a "people interests" which provide substantial economic benefits to the US through a variety of leakages associated with high import content, tourism and the provisions of a ready and steady supply of cheap labor, professional and other skilled workers.

Just as importantly Caribbean people, via the Cuba connection, constitute a coniferous and critical lobby" within the US to which the government might not always defer but equally cannot ignore electorally.

While vital security and economic interests provide a tangible basis for distinction of policy in the region they are nevertheless conducted within the scope of inter American policy.

Following the invasion of Domingo Republic 1965 and the aftermath ending an activist phrase, the US lowered its profile toward Latin America and the Caribbean but not necessarily Central America.

Under Nixon, Ford – Kissinger administration concerns were limited to specific cases – Chile 1970 – 1973 and Ford 1975 – 1978 rather than expressed and pronounced policies.

The CBI i.e. The Caribbean Basin Initiative launched by President Reagan 02-24-82 did much injustice to the Caribbean people.

It came about largely in part by the efforts of a number of Prime Ministers in the Commonwealth such as Edward Seaga of Jamaica amongst others who needed a strong US presence in the region because of the Castro fear of friendliness towards many of our so-called leaders who were scared of dealing with Castro.

President Reagan used security and economic assistance as a draw to prop up these governments who used the funds mainly for security apparatus and purchase heavy arms.

Other confrontations developed, for example in Central America, El Salvador was to be seen favorably and Honduras or Belize not highly strategic (Was that because of the African nature of the people?) That's an issue we will debate later.

While in English speaking countries Jamaica, and the Easter Caribbean States members were deemed worthy of massive economic assistance, notably due to the situation of the instability in Grenada.

All plans specifically excluded Maurice Bishop partisans in Grenada for any assistance resulting in much chaos and damage to the Grenadian economic forecast.

The double standards used in the CBI was extensively unpopular from Nassau to Kingston or Port a Spain along with friends and foes alike.

Even though in 1982 Eugenia Charles declared "The Caribbean has been expecting action on this program since 1981. Our peoples will say to the US, "The US are talkers and not doers."

And even Sir Lynden Pindling said, "If Cuba is worth nine million dollars a day to the Russians, how much is the Caribbean/Bahamas for the USA?

If Russia for three and a quarter billion dollars a day for the Russians to underwrite the cost of insurrect in the region. How far would the USA go to the preservation of peace and security in the region"?

Well put.

The CBI to the Republicans (USA) reflected simply their belief that the region as a theater of East West conflict matters, which most of the Caribbean and Bahamas people did not concur with.

The Bahamas Trinidad, Belize and Guyana amongst others have been opposed to the US military intervention in the region. But since most of these countries gained independence from Britain it became mandatory to deal with the Americans for greater participations and protection since most of these countries cannot patrol the ocean surrounding the Caribbean seas appropriately.

Long before independence these nations always tolerated acceptance of the American even in the light of the people wish to remain "Nonaligned" as expressed in the UN by Bahamas and Belizean vote.

Many countries have suffered economically because of these positions taken at the UN by our representatives.

Other confrontations developed either overtly or covertly by the USA operatives - example: (DEA- CIA- Other unnamed actors – Other)

Amongst other nations with a keen interest in the affairs of the Caribbean was presidents of Mexico and Venezuela both members of the OPEC bloc.

1980 the San Jose Agreement (SJA) agreed to supply the oil consumption of Caribbean nations on concessionaire terms. in 1981 they agreed to meet with the USA and Canada in the Bahamas to further resolve and coordination of aid provisions in the region and sought unsuccessfully 1to persuade the US president to take a less militaristic approach when dealing with the region but they tried.

Indeed, in the view of president Echeverria successor Mexico president Lopez Portillo 1981 was vital in terms of coordination and cooperation between Venezuela and Mexico to achieve the stability of the 28 nations of the CBI region.

The Bahamas is in itself from 1973 – to present as articulated in foreign policy statements recently ostentatiously prides itself as part Atlantic and part Caribbean.

Now newer markets must be planted and grow CARICOM, CSME and others have to step up and advocate with a greater voice for the children and future of this region to be protected and flourish for the good of all our children and people in the future.

Why MICAL Must Have a Seat In Parliament

To the Leadership of the Progressive Liberal Party, To the People of MICAL, and To All Who Believe in Representation Rooted in Soil and Service:

We, the undersigned advocates for justice, dignity, and authentic representation, raise our voices in firm opposition to the nomination of a wealthy, non-indigenous individual seeking to represent the MICAL constituency under the PLP banner.

MICAL is not a trophy seat. It is a sacred trust—comprised of Mayaguana, Inagua, Crooked Island, Acklins, and Long Cay—each bearing the scars of neglect and the brilliance of resilience. Our communities have long been sidelined in national development conversations, and we cannot afford another cycle of parachuted leadership that lacks lived experience, ancestral ties, or sustained service to our people.

We do not oppose wealth. We oppose the commodification of representation. We do not oppose outsiders. We oppose opportunism.

This appeal is not personal—it is proportional. It reflects the decades of sacrifice made by MICAL's youth, elders, farmers, teachers, and cultural stewards who have built movements from the ground up. It honors the legacy of P. Carl Gibson, Edmund Moxey, and others who were sidelined not for lack of vision, but for refusing to "play the game."

We call on the PLP to uphold its stated values of inclusion, transparency, and grassroots empowerment. Let MICAL speak for MICAL. Let the soil choose its steward.

Respectfully, Deliverance Campaign for MICAL Dignity

We Are MICAL: A Declaration of Dignity and Demands

We are the children of Mayaguana, Inagua, Crooked Island, and Acklins—descendants of those displaced after Hurricane Donna, evicted not just by wind and water, but by silence and neglect. We speak now, not in whispers, but with the full force of memory and vision.

The sanitized candidates of the FNM parading through our islands with polished shoes and no promises to upgrade or do XYZ Or This or That. They are toothless in the face of real policy. Where is the blueprint for food security? For hurricane-resilient housing? For national development that includes us— not just in name, but in infrastructure, education, and opportunity?

The USA's space programs may have had an affect on MICAL indirectly or not. Yet we are treated as footnotes in our own story. We demand procurement plans, not platitudes.

The former MP from Bain Town has shown no appetite for the hard work of transformation. He floats on the blessings of party hierarchy, doing the easy work while the hard truths rot beneath the surface. Pintard, meanwhile, treats this as a skit— surrounded by preppy actors, rehearsing lines that never reach our shores.

But we are not props. We are not extras. We are MICAL Islanders with ideas, with plans, with a vision for growth rooted in soil and soul.

We want:

- Universal health insurance

- Schools that uplift, not abandon

- A platter of opportunity that belongs to every child—not parceled out by party or pedigree

No one made this country. God gave it to all of us. In peace and security, we shall ride together—or fall apart.

We reject the lipstick and flossy smiles. We want architects of justice, not actors of illusion.

We Are MICAL: A Declaration of Dignity and Demands

We are the children of Mayaguana, Inagua, Crooked Island, and Acklins—descendants of those displaced after Hurricane Donna, evicted not just by wind and water, but by silence and neglect. We speak now, not in whispers, but with the full force of memory and vision.

The sanitized candidates of the FNM parading through our islands with polished shoes and no promises to upgrade or do XYZ Or This or That. They are toothless in the face of real policy. Where is the blueprint for food security? For hurricane-resilient housing? For national development that includes us— not just in name, but in infrastructure, education, and opportunity?

The USA's space programs affect MICAL directly. Yet we are treated as footnotes in our own story. We demand procurement plans, not platitudes.

The former MP from Bain Town has shown no appetite for the hard work of transformation. He floats on the blessings of party hierarchy, doing the easy work while the hard truths rot beneath the surface. Pintard, meanwhile, treats this as a skit—surrounded by preppy actors, rehearsing lines that never reach our shores.

But we are not props. We are not extras. We are MICAL Islanders with ideas, with plans, with a vision for growth rooted in soil and soul.

We want:

- Universal health insurance

- Schools that uplift, not abandon

- A platter of opportunity that belongs to every child—not parceled out by .party or pedigree

No one made this country. God gave it to all of us. In peace and security, we shall ride together—or fall apart.

We reject the lipstick and flossy smiles. We want architects of justice, not actors of illusion.

+++++++++++++++++++++

1971 Summer at the National Archives

After completing classes at the Teacher's College of The Bahamas in Oakes Field, as a young, unemployed, and eager to contribute—visited the Ministry of Education & Culture. A high school friend suggested he apply for work at the newly formed National Archives on Mackey Street, overseen by Gail Saunders.

Gibson was hired, but instead of being trained in archival work, he was repeatedly assigned menial outdoor tasks. Shirley Burrows, acting under Saunders' auspices, would instruct him to "go outside and sweep up the fallen limbs from the large trees near the side of the road." Despite his protests and requests to learn about the Archives' purpose and function, he was consistently sidelined. Gail Saunders reportedly responded, "Just keep the side of the road sweep clean."

Gibson interpreted this treatment as exclusionary and possibly gender-biased, noting Saunders' preference for female staff and her apparent disregard for his intellectual curiosity. He eventually left the post, disheartened by the lack of mentorship and opportunity.

This experience—largely undocumented in official histories—reveals the early post-independence tensions around access, institutional gatekeeping, and the marginalization of young Bahamian men in cultural spaces. It also marks a formative moment in Gibson's lifelong commitment to reclaiming national dignity and challenging erasure.

Gibson was always eager to find ways to make the islands more favorable for islanders, championing practical reforms and cultural pride. But the gatekeepers of the PLP ensured that certain roles and responsibilities were reserved for select individuals—often those who conformed to unwritten codes of loyalty and performance. Gibson, not fitting the mold of a "player," was sidelined—his potential overlooked by a system that favored conformity over innovation and appearance over substance.

++++++++++++++++

Carl's Plans for MICAL

How $31 million could transform the MICAL islands (Mayaguana, Inagua, Crooked Island, Acklins, and Long Cay) through food security, education, disaster readiness, and direct economic support and through the trade routes could generate additional funds for further development.

Budget Breakdown: $31 Million for MICAL Transformation

Initiative	Budget (USD)	Description
Agricultural Development	$8,000,000	Establish 5 island-based farms with irrigation, greenhouses, training, and co-ops for trade/export
Education & School Exchange	$4,200,000	Hire 40+ teachers, upgrade schools, and launch West Indies school exchange program
Early Warning & Disaster Resilience	$3,500,000	Install sirens, weather stations, satellite comms, shelters, and community training
Stimulus Checks for Voting-Age Adults	$11,780,000	$380 per person for ~31,000 residents (est. voting-age population across MICAL)
Program Management & Oversight	$2,520,000	Local staffing, audits, logistics, and contingency (~8% of total budget)
TOTAL	$31,000,000	100% allocated with measurable impact

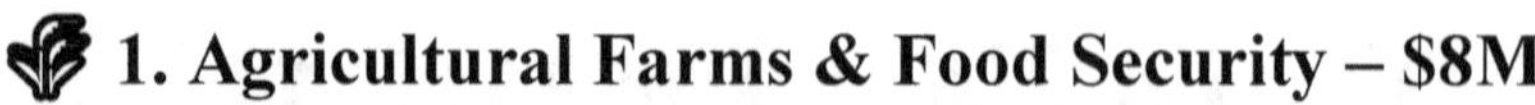

1. Agricultural Farms & Food Security – $8M

Goal: Feed local communities, reduce imports, create jobs, and export to other islands.

What's included:

- **5 island farms** (1 per island) with:
  - Greenhouses, irrigation, composting, cold storage
  - Livestock pens (goats, chickens), aquaponics systems
- **Training programs** for 100+ residents in farming, agro-processing, and business
- **Co-op model** for selling to schools, hotels, and inter-island trade
- **Mobile farmers' markets** and refrigerated transport

Sample allocation:

- Infrastructure & equipment: $5.2M
- Training & staffing: $1.2M
- Transport & logistics: $0.8M
- Marketing & co-op setup: $0.8M

2. Education & School Exchange – $4.2M

Goal: Improve local education and connect MICAL students with peers across the Caribbean.

What's included:

- **Hire 40+ teachers** across MICAL (math, science, agriculture, languages)
- **Upgrade 10 schools** with internet, labs, and learning materials
- **West Indies School Exchange Program**:
  - Virtual classrooms, cultural exchanges, student travel grants
- **Teacher housing stipends** and retention bonuses

Sample allocation:

- Teacher salaries (2 years): $2.4M
- School upgrades: $1.2M
- Exchange program: $0.4M
- Housing & bonuses: $0.2M

3. Early Warning & Disaster Resilience – $3.5M

Goal: Protect lives and property with real-time alerts and community readiness.

What's included:

- **Sirens and weather stations** in each settlement
- **Satellite phones and radios** for emergency teams
- **Community shelters** with backup power and water
- **Training programs** for disaster response and first aid

Sample allocation:

- Equipment & installation: $2.2M

- Shelter upgrades: $0.8M

- Training & outreach: $0.5M

🏧 4. Stimulus Checks – $11.78M

Goal: Direct economic support to every voting-age adult in MICAL.

Assumptions:

- Estimated **31,000 voting-age residents** across the 5 islands

- Each receives **$380** one-time stimulus

Distribution:

- Via local banks, post offices, or mobile money platforms

- Verification through voter registry and ID

👦💼 5. Program Management & Oversight – $2.52M

Goal: Ensure transparency, local hiring, and successful delivery.

What's included:

- **Local project managers** and coordinators

- **Audits and reporting** every 6 months

- **Community boards** for oversight and feedback

- **Contingency fund** for inflation or emergencies

☑ What Residents Would See

- Fresh produce and meats grown locally

- Better schools, more teachers, and cultural exchanges

- Real-time alerts and safe shelters during storms

- $380 in their pocket to spend, save, or invest

- Jobs in farming, education, logistics, and maintenance

++++++++++++++++++++++++++++++

Sample Letter to the Editor

The Editor:

Could you share my sentiment on this matter to the general public?

In memory of the great and awesome forefathers who spoke to the people and placed before us all, what made this land a 'Commonwealth jewel' and stop the violent against one another and tame the gate keeping for the political parties. Echoes of 'this land is our land...this land is your land from Matthew town Inagua all the way to the Bimimi island', now it is true we are no more "subjects" of the Crown. At some point we got to find a resolution and stop the tearing down and build up every one of these Out Island municipalities going forward and secure the "deed or title" for every one of the indigenous children and people of this land going into the future. Islanders cannot be replaced and forgotten as some forefathers and foremothers farmed and toiled to make the land a "Better" inclusive place for all to live.

+++++++++

Crime Prevention in Bahamas

Crime Prevention Plan for the Islands of the Bahamas (Effective 2026)

This plan draws inspiration from the visionary work of P. Carl Gibson and aims to address the root causes of crime through cultural dignity, economic justice, and community healing. It is designed to be inclusive, restorative, and forward-looking, with a special focus on historically marginalized communities across the Bahamian archipelago.

1. Equitable Development in Out Islands

- Prioritize infrastructure projects in the MICAL Islands (Mayaguana, Inagua, Crooked Island, Acklins, and Long Cay)

- Expand access to libraries, clinics, schools, and youth centers

- Launch "Build Where We Belong" initiatives to foster local pride and opportunity

2. Cultural Identity and Civic Education

- Integrate Bahamian history and civic education into school curricula

- Highlight contributions of overlooked national figures like Edmund Moxey, Arthur Hanna, and Bulla Danny

- Promote cultural programming that reinforces respect, responsibility, and belonging

3. Institutional Accountability

- Enact whistleblower protections and anti-retaliation policies

- Audit ministries for misuse of power and ensure transparency

- Train public servants in ethical governance and community engagement

4. Community Healing and Truth Forums

- Establish regional Truth Forums to address historical injustices

- Facilitate storytelling, testimony, and reconciliation processes

- Support mental health services and trauma-informed care

5. Economic Justice and Land Access

- Provide land grants to Out Island families for farming and housing

- Support cooperatives, small-scale agriculture, and local entrepreneurship

- Ensure fair wages and protections for cultural workers and educators

6. Youth Empowerment and Crime Prevention Programs

- Launch mentorship, apprenticeship, and job training programs

- Create safe spaces for youth expression, sports, and arts

- Partner with churches, NGOs, and community leaders to guide at-risk youth

7. Data-Driven Policing and Public Safety

- Implement community policing models with local oversight

- Use data to identify crime hotspots and deploy resources strategically

- Train officers in de-escalation, cultural sensitivity, and restorative justice

8. Regional Connectivity and Caribbean Travel Links (2027)

- Develop direct air routes between MICAL airports and Caribbean capitals such as Kingston, Port of Spain, Bridgetown, and Santo Domingo

- Partner with regional airlines and tourism ministries to establish affordable and reliable service

- Upgrade airport facilities in MICAL Islands to meet international standards and support customs and immigration processing

- Promote cultural exchange and economic cooperation through inter-island travel initiatives

Public Statement to Caribbean Ministries

We no longer wait behind grey curtains. We open the gates from MICAL to the Caribbean, not as beggars—but as builders.

We extend our hands in partnership, rooted in dignity and shared history. The people of the MICAL Islands seek not charity, but collaboration—built on mutual respect, cultural exchange, and economic justice.

Let this be the beginning of a new era of regional unity, where our airports become gateways of opportunity, our youth ambassadors of peace, and our communities' co-authors of Caribbean progress.

Together, we rise beyond borders. Together, we build beyond curtains.

We welcome inclusivity and dialogue.

In the spirit of MICAL force grace be with you.

++++++++++++++

PM meets U.S.A President.

Reaffirming that there is no justification for the United States to name The Bahamas in a stop taxation bill, Prime Minister the Rt. Hon. Hubert Ingraham said The Bahamas does not expect that its name will appear in such legislation at the end of the day.

At the 5th Summit of the Americas in Port of Spain, Trinidad Saturday, leaders of the Caribbean Community (Caricom) met with members of the US House of Representatives Financial Services Committee and a Congressional delegation led by Chairman of the House Ways and Means Committee Charles Rangel and Chairman of the Western Hemisphere Subcommittee Eliot Engel on the United States' Stop Tax Haven Abuse Act.

The initiative is an effort to prevent US citizens from using offshore jurisdictions to avoid or evade paying taxes owed to the US government. Such an initiative could affect The Bahamas to the extent that legislation including The Bahamas on a list of countries regarded as tax havens could negatively affect the country's reputation as a place to invest and do business.

Mr. Ingraham said, "The US Congressmen were not able to provide a justification for [The Bahamas being named]. There is no justification for the Americans to put The Bahamas in a stop taxation Bill - the facts do not square with that. We expect therefore that at the end of the day our name will not appear in any such legislation."

Prime Minister Ingraham said he previously wrote to Congressman Rangel on The Bahamas' position, and had also written on behalf of Caricom at the Community's request.

"I think he gave us sufficient assurances about the Bill to cause most of our members to be comfortable," Mr. Ingraham advised. "There will be some additional discussions with the Congress."

Calling the stop taxation initiative "misguided" insofar as The Bahamas is concerned, Prime Minister Ingraham explained: "We have cooperated with the United States fully, we have a tax information exchange agreement with them, the Treasury Department and the Internal Revenue Service (IRS) would all certify that all requests made in The Bahamas have been responded to appropriately."

Mr. Ingraham advised that negotiations on a Tax Information Exchange Agreement (TIEA) with Canada and other countries are currently underway.

Caricom met in bilateral talks with Canadian Prime Minister Stephen Harper on Saturday. During those talks, Prime Minister Harper announced that Canada would make 160 additional scholarships for Caribbean students to study at colleges and universities there."

Thank you Sir.

++++++++++++++++++

Riding the Frezel

Good morning every day we sat in the small kitchen room and monitored the activities that was happen close to the shores of Acklins and Crooked islands ony to see two vessels that had signs in another language that was not English, so we proceeded to track them down and there they were hiding behind the smaller cays close up to the rock covered with a fatiqe color clothings.

That was an early morning in Sept 1975 we had encountered the fishig boat hauling in heavy nets filled with fishes.

What were we to do?

Big boat with people that maybve spoke little English and may be armed so we kept og headed to the island of Mayaguana and wrote down what was seen.

++++++++++++++++

ImagineBahamasBeyond2026

Grand Design for the New Bahamas, the Patriots/Fathers talked about.

Here are the facts as they are known:

Look inside the country

Look all around the islands

The islands are changing fast

But moving to where?

But moving to where?

Imagine Bahamas with a Patriotic Nationalist government and a forward i.e. FORWARD looking Administration that initiates a SAED economic development agenda – i.e. Shock & Awe Economic Development (SAED).

With decades of sovereignty the grand design "THEY" i.e. the PATRIOTS talked about.

The Bahamas finally begin advances into the 21 century with three (3) Administrative Divisions to comprise the new Bahamas.

The three (3) AD (Administrative Divisions) named as follows:

N.B

Northern Administrative Division namely the islands of Grand Bahama, Abaco, Berry islands, ________________________

Central Administrative Division namely New Providence, Exuma, San Salvador, Cat island, ________________________

Southern Administrative Division namely the islands of MICAL i.e., Mayaguana, Inagua, Acklins, Crooked island and Long Cay, ___________________________________

Note well Each island with a legitimate Member of Parliament and a Senator who will no longer be appointed but elected by the people for the people and to do the peoples work.

Effectively electing a new Prime Minister who competes for election democratically on a fixed and certain day, date and time.

Example: Second Tuesday of May every five (5) years and election for the office of Prime Minister; Persons filed from known and unknown political organizations, parties. All are welcome to participate.

House of Assembly members, elections same as it always been, however, new will be elections will be fixed to a set date and day every five (5) years example Wednesday of August unless otherwise specified example – collapse of a government as result of a " no confidence" vote or other national emergencies unknown as this time.

The Prime Minister appoints who He/She deems fit to serve the good of the country as outlined by the political machinery of his/her alignment in a smarter smaller cabinet column.

(n.b) The Governor General will no longer be as we know it to be from 1460 to the present.

The Governor General will be simply a reminder of the past no longer will there be a "Speech from the Throne" but a "Speech" called; " The State of the Nation,: or " State of the State," speech.

Government House will be useful for a) National museum and or b) Act as a guest house for visiting Diplomats and other personalities and the like.

The cabinet comprised of the following:

1 Deputy Prime Minister. 1 Attorney General.

2 Deputy Attorney Generals. Each assigned to or primarily to each of the new Administrative Division to deal specifically with issues associated with matter relative to " eminent domain " – Island Rights – land distribution or land re-distribution and other pertinent issues to be outlined as deemed along with criminal, liability, ________________,

________________, ________________.

Prime Minister to set up smaller/smarter cabinet to execute the countries' business to include a newly named Minister of the Interior – Finance – Education – Health – Labor – Trade – Defense – Transportation – Tourism – Foreign Affairs – Inter-island Affairs – Culture .

Imagine Bahamas Beyond 2026 with a government that implements a rational and well understood Bahamianization policy –market (CM)

Solution / resolution to the human trade (boat people) migration/ immigration matters.

Integration to a cohesive common market (cm)

Indigenous people land distribution

Trade policy understood and outlined with Caribbean countries/ South America / Asia/ European Union/ Africa/ USA/ Eastern European countries.

Imagine Bahamas beyond 2026 (IBB2026) with a patriotic nationalist government that set up and establishes a functional people oriented regime with the following for the betterment of the people:

a) S.O.R.S (Strategic Oil Reserve Suply) The minimize the lack of petroleum throughout the territories and the maintenance /regulation of fair pricing & market stability.

b) B.M.T.S (Bahamas Maritime Tracking System) i.e. Installed I all mailboats etc plying the national waters.

c) N.C.M (National Cellular market – deregulation and opening cellular services to competition.

d) I.I.A.T (Inter island Air Transportation.

e) I.I.T.B (Inter island tourism board.

f) New postal rates for mass mailers/advertisers/bulk mailers.

g) Housing department that renders residents a helping hand not a hand-out.

h) B.T.A. (Bahamas Transportation Authority) A semi – quasi agency that administers the mass movement of people in New Providence island and throughout the island nation.

i) National Prescription Drug plan to ensure the pricing of imported drugs may be cost effective and more reasonable.

j) No more free lancer ministers in the name of the people these Bahamas Islands.

Any government in these Bahamas is to begin and move quickly on establishing a guideline that outlines the following for the people of this nation:

These are the things we were talking about:

End the human rights crisis in the Bahamas by forever Halting the Solitary confinement of prisoners who does not deserve such treatment.

Establish well publicized community announcements that deal with the ingrained vice(s) with xenophobia and work to promote racial equality among the people embracing national consciousness and purpose and duty.

- Enact a living wage for ALL Bahamians, so all who work hard may grow and thrive

- Set up a well-defined Freedom of Information Act for the people.

- Reform the Criminal Justice System so that it represents everyone's life and shared existence – equally

- Strengthen the rent laws of the islands – Protect tenants, end vacancy decontrol and provide affordable homes for all people.

- Establish or re-negotiate a pact with CARICOM countries that takes into account the migrant issues that is affecting the islands of the Bahamas and set up a Satellite center on an assigned island that deals exclusively with the Haitian, Cuban and other islands from poverty stricken Caribbean nations that flocks to the islands of the Bahamas.

- Appoint new and assertive Bahamian conscious Ambassadors that represent the attractive vital interests of the islands of the Bahamas in Trade with China, USA, Canada, Mexico, Jamaica and other countries to be identified in the New Year i.e. 2022 and beyond.

- Stop the sale of native lands to foreigners coming to the Bahamas who have been allowed to buy out the local inhabitants of MICAL islands, Cat island, Andros, Berry islands, Long island, Sal Salvador and other islands to be named in 2016.

- To take back all the properties that is called "Crown land" that has been sold to questionable people.

- Establish forth rightly a Civilian Complaint Board that hears the issues associated with police abuses and the likes.

Set up a Reconciliation framework that will resolve long hidden issues associated with political discrimination of the early years of independence.

- The breakup of the MICAL islands to have duly elected members of parliament for each island i.e., Mayaguana, Inagua, Acklin's, Crooked islands and Long Cay.

- Finally to have members of the Bahamas senate to BE ELECTED by the people and not appointed by the party that won the election to have a term not longer than 4 years interval before calling election thereof.

- Establish an Inter-island Tourism Board.

- Installed in all commercial fishing boats, mail boats and ships that ply the waters of the Bahamas a device that is used to identify readily by the local authorities for a marginal fee. Also, this will enhance national security broadly for the islands.

- Setup a comprehensive public transportation system in the Bahamas to be called The Bahamas Metro Transportation System (BMTS)

- N.C.M (National Cellular market – deregulation and opening cellular services to competition. d) I.I.A.T (Inter island Air Transportation. e) I.I.T.B (Inter island tourism board.   f)   New   postal   rates   for   mass mailers/advertisers/bulk mailers.

The above mentioned would not take five (5) years to implement. But the process must begin ASAP so "we" the people would begin to believe that this Brave/Cooper regime is a true progressive thing for this country.

- Peace be unto All the Brothers and Sisters everywhere.

- Thank you for your SUPPORT.

++++++++++++++

Besty Bay Dreaming

My hope is with moderate ideas, advancing for the growth of the country, each island having the same voting right in parliament to advocate for continuity and balance for the indigenous folks who are becoming a vanishing minority, in a country where our fatherfathers and mothers paced and paid for, against the invading merchants, colonial masters and the political imposters.

"We the people" have to start somewhere, unequivocally to jostle the hate and sorrow over the pain the people have been allowed to suffer, for these many years.

Let the the people live with dignity and economic fairness to florish. **Bahamas & Island territories: Cannot keep lowering the threshold.**

Wider dialogue is pivotally commendable but at the end of the day, it is suggested when matters are relating to the national security and peace of the nation many more voices should be heard. Continuum of blocking voices that are different in totality and concept is adversarial for national stability and maintenance of order.

++++++++++++

Assorted Bahamas Stories 2020

Did you know in 1955 Mayaguana had 1708 people on the island?

Did you know August 12 1969 - June 12,1972 another 250 people left because the land where they had farmed produced little following hurricane season where Camille devastated the landscape of western Cuba

And the southeastern region of the Bahamas took a beating and many homes and personal items were destroyed and washed away by the water to never been seen again.

Recalled 1975

When Prime minister Lynden O. Pindling recreated the spark that was new to the children of the 1960's following the Bay of Pigs drama many young people in the outer islanders was really excited that now we may have a voice in what and who be coming to the country saying they our friends and protectors.

That was what many people thought.

But the Bahamas out islanders knew well, someone had to tell the story of why Cuban and Russian patriots roaming on the islands of the Bahamas was amazing. While many people asked why was U.S.A president Kennedy making such a fuss, with American navy ships and frigates everywhere around Mayaguana and the region?

So, Sir Lynden O. Pindling ignited the light and brought them hope from the indolence of Sir Stafford Sands and Sir Roland Symonette in the 1950's and 1960's.

All of these notes were taken when papa was on the Cape Hatteras headed with Brucie Taylor back to Nassau Bahamas from the island of Mayaguana Besty Bay coast, to bring back food supplies to Mayaguana and sometimes maybe sometime to Acklins island.

By now many older islanders had already left and headed to Freeport Grand Bahamas because there was, "big development" headed to those islands in the north. Sir Stafford Sands and the vagarious Sir Roland Symonette was not playing they was about making loot for their clans.

Bahamas & Island history as recalled before the crackdown 1967, my sister and her 'holy than thou' religious husband had been appointed to lead a chapel in Matthew town Inagua and that was supposed to be a "miracle', coming from Pirates Well, Mayaguana where we had to walk long distance to fetch water to bath and drink sometimes take the horses to the well was a chore no one wanted to do but it was one of the chores some elders pin on the young lads to do.

But then the telephone started ringing and that was a miracle too, back in 1966, you had to go to the Commissioner's office to whine up the phone and call up our relatives on Palm Beach Street in New Providence Island to tell them the mail boat was coming and someone had something for them to go to Porter's cay dock and pick it up.

================================

Beloved Looking Back

Do not human beings have a hard labor on earth

And are not their days like the days of a laborer?

Like a hard worker who longs for the shade

And like laborers who look for their salaries?

So I am allotted months of emptiness

And nights of misery are apportioned to me?

When I lie down I say,

"When shall I awake?

But the night is long and I am full

of tossing until dawn..

My days are swifter than a weaver's shuttle.

The lament of Job in the days long before any one was here.

Job 7, 1 - 6.

This too shall pass beloved.

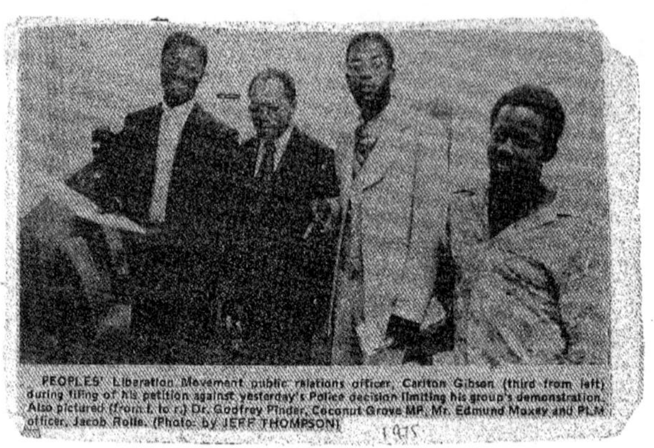

Proof of the political discrimination and punishment for voicing an opinion with relevant leaders of that time

Crime Prevention Plan for the Islands of the Bahamas (Effective 2026)

This plan draws inspiration from the visionary work of P. Carl Gibson and aims to address the root causes of crime through cultural dignity, economic justice, and community healing. It is designed to be inclusive, restorative, and forward-looking, with a special focus on historically marginalized communities across the Bahamian archipelago.

With clarity and conviction about this before, Behind Grey Curtains wasn't just reactive—it was restorative emphasizing that the "blitz" of crime in New Providence isn't just a policing issue, but a **cultural and structural emergency**. Here's a distilled reminder of the approach:

Getting Ready FIPP -Framework for Addressing Crime in New Providence

1. Reclaim the Narrative

- Rejection of the sensationalism and deficit framing in Nassau media regurgitated.

- Called for **community-led storytelling** that dignifies neighborhoods like "Over the Hill," rather than criminalizing them.

2. Mobilize Cultural Infrastructure

- Proposed **murals, anthems, and youth forums** as tools to reclaim public space and memory.

- Emphasized that **beauty and belonging** are crime deterrents when rooted in local soil.

3. Truth Forums & Curtain Marches

- Set up and put together **intergenerational gatherings** where elders and youth confront the trauma of violence and erasure.

- These aren't just symbolic—they're meant to **restore emotional literacy and civic trust**.

4. Strategic Pressure on Institutions

- Demanded **transparency in bail reform**, especially for repeat offenders.

- Called for **Freedom of Information enforcement** to track funding, policing, and justice outcomes.

5. Build from the Bottom Up

- Championed **Out Island youth empowerment** as a long-term antidote to urban despair.

- Advocate that **MICAL, Exuma, and Eleuthera** must be spotlighted—not just as escape routes, but as **models of dignity and resilience**.

6. Protect the Protectors

- Insisted that **youth leaders and cultural workers** must be shielded from co-optation and retaliation.

+++++++++++++++++++++++++++

Dada True that

I recalled saying since as a little boychild, in 1969, some years after the missionary doctor did the medical miracle procedure on his left eye from complications with his eyesight Mayaguana shall rise.

Behind Grey Curtains by P. Carl Gibson, was not only real it was and still is hitting hard, masses of the Over the Hill people and especially the Out Islanders.

Even on Sunday, the Sunday school teacher was making deals with the political people for who she like and who she did not like for jobs? True stories to top it all, is this pivotal story about gender i.ds?

Ms. Knowles echoed succinctly; "I was told I'd never be promoted because I was an unwed single mother," years before Royal Bahamas Police Force (RBPF) now, Commissioner Shanta Knowles was promoted to the highest post on the force, she said she was told that, as a single mother, she would never advance in her career.

This deserves to be woven into the very spine of *Behind Grey Curtains*—not as a footnote, but as a living echo of the truths P. Carl Gibson has been voicing since 1969. Here's how we might frame it, with dignity and clarity, in a way that honors both the historical arc and the emotional resonance:

📑 *Behind Grey Curtains — A* Living Testament

From the mailboat migrations of the 1950s to the whispered betrayals in Sunday school pews, *Behind Grey Curtains* is not just a book—it's a mirror held up to a nation still wrestling with its conscience. P. Carl Gibson's work, rooted in the lived experiences of Over-the-Hill communities and Out Islanders, exposes the quiet deals, the systemic exclusions, and the spiritual contradictions that have shaped Bahamian life for decades.

Even in sanctuaries meant for moral instruction, political favoritism crept in—Sunday school teachers brokering employment based on personal allegiances rather than merit. These were not isolated incidents. They were symptoms of a broader malaise: a society where dignity was conditional, and justice was often delayed.

And then, there is the reported account of Commissioner Shanta Knowles. Before she shattered another glass ceilings as the first female Commissioner of the Royal Bahamas Police Force, she was told she'd never be promoted—simply because she was an unwed single mother. Her rise is not just a personal triumph; it's a rebuke to the gendered gatekeeping that *Behind Grey Curtains* MICAL Confidential has long documented. Knowles' journey from Rock Sound, Eleuthera to the highest rank in law enforcement is a testament to the very resilience Gibson has chronicled for generations

Behind Grey Curtains MICAL Confidential is smoothly paced, intelligent and intricately plastered with remarkable and conclusive ideas and details of how a young country could embrace all its citizens moving forward with uniquely progressive and predictably stunning ways the nation could shine forth with balanced economic and social growth for all the people. P. Carl Gibson aka

Ammadou is indeed a brilliant storyteller of the history of the new and independent nation, which thrived minimally to grow and or equally parcel out with fairness to all residents, where equilibrium should be praised and admired. Yellow Elder would shine again; while with revolutionary leanings, P. Carl Gibson aka Ammadou divulged himself from the neocolonial and classic demeanor vertiginously displayed by the political operatives towards islanders from the then known Out islands who'd been compelled to migrate to New Providence and Freeport, Grand Bahama for a piece of the developing pie. Even though many who did not benefit from the pie that was carved up immediately following the July 10th 1973 political separation from London, England, the tribal instrument that surfaced sought out those who had tasted freedom of speech and assembly for the first time with varying degrees of bamboozlement and isolation. In 1972 the islands of the Bahamas some fear had penetrated the culture; he'd sought to integrate into a formula where progress and positive thinking for national movement could give birth. P. Carl Gibson aka Ammadou wondered out loudly what was becoming of the nation when the people no longer communicated rationally with each other. Then he'd caught the whim of how again some local leaders literally directed partisans with venom and expletives had become an acceptable usage of communication. But he was reminded of what was before and what he'd been propelled into. For he had no knowledge he was going to write or what he would write about. But then Behind Grey Curtains was among the many essays he compiled as a personal history of things he'd gone through as a new and independent national.

As a product of the enlightened mail boat era 1959-1975, he traveled the so-called "Hell's gate" passage on the Frezel and the many other mail boats owned by the Taylors of Pirates Well Mayaguana, Bahamas on his way to New Providence; doing exactly what many patriots before had encountered while breaking the mold of the traditional role a teacher played in 1974 New Providence Bahamas.

About The Author

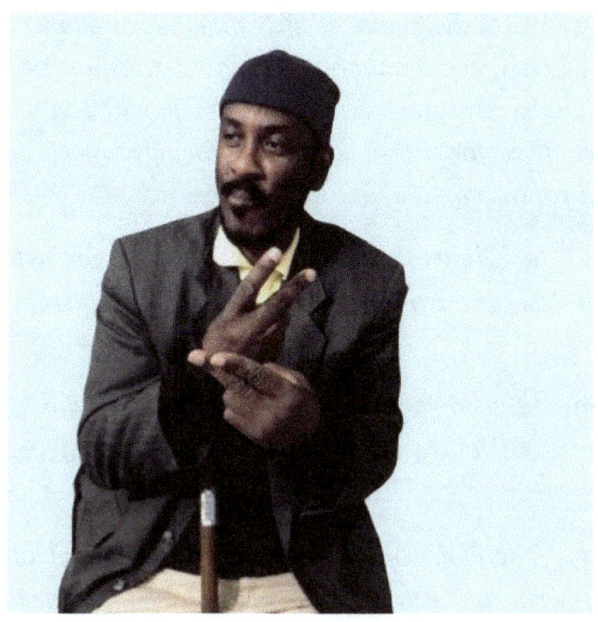

A Quiet Meeting in Nassau – 1975

Setting: A modest office in Nassau. The walls are lined with photographs of Junkanoo parades and youth choirs. A fan hums overhead. Gibson, freshly returned from Mayaguana using the mailboat Cape Hatteras captained by Bruce Taylor with his assistant Bulla Danny. P. Carl Gibson sits across from Moxey, who's reviewing a folder of community proposals.

Gibson: *"Mr. Moxey, I've come not with complaints—but with a vision. Mayaguana and Inagua are not forgotten lands. They are the soul of our people. But the young men there— they're leaving. Not because they want to, but because they must."*

Moxey: *"I know that story too well. Grants Town, Bain Town—we've fought for dignity here. But the Out Islands? They've been left behind in the rush."*

Gibson: *"Exactly. We need investment, yes—but more than that, we need respect. A mail boat isn't just transport. It's lifeline. A youth choir isn't just music. It's memory. I'm asking for cultural centers, for mural walls, for forums where elders can speak and youths can listen."*

Moxey: *(nodding slowly) "You're asking for what every Bahamian deserves. Not charity. Not spectacle. Just a chance to be seen."*

Gibson: *"And to stay home with pride. If we don't act now, the curtains will close on their stories. And we'll be left with silence."*

Moxey: *"Then let's open them. I'll bring this to Cabinet. But you—keep writing. Keep speaking. The Out Islands need a voice. And I think it's yours."*

Gibson ***"Thanks greatly. But do you think other mailboats might be able to facilitate any transfers for the people of Mayaguana and Inagua?'***

Moxey: "I will get back to you and others about what may be likely done".

That final comment was how Moxey always look out for the people that needed a little help.